SALADS FROM AROUND THE WORLD

GETTING IT RIGHT

SALADS FROM AROUND THE WORLD

by Judy Ridgway & Carolyn Humphries

foulsham

LONDON • NEW YORK • TORONTO • SYDNEY

foulsham

The Publishing House
Bennetts Close, Cippenham, Berks SL1 5AP

ISBN 0-572-02138-0

Phototypeset in Great Britain by Typesetting Solutions, Slough, Berks.
Printed in Great Britain by Cox & Wyman Ltd., Reading, Berks.

CONTENTS

INTRODUCTION

When I first became interested in making and eating salads I found that there was a distinct gap in most recipe books at this point. A few basic recipes for coleslaw or tomato salad and that was that.

Today, the situation has changed significantly and salads have become universally popular. The recipes for salads are increasingly inventive and international in character.

You do not have to be a health fanatic to enjoy salads. Nor do you have to be addicted to the proverbial 'rabbit food', though for those who are interested, recipes containing only raw food are included.

All sorts of ingredients can be brought into service, varying from cold cooked meats and fish, through fruits and nuts to every obtainable kind of vegetable.

This book is packed with ideas for everything from starters to side salads, main courses to desserts. And it is also intended to stimulate you into trying out your own ideas based on your likes and dislikes and on the contents of your fridge and store cupboard.

Ingredients, Preparation and Storage

• All the recipes are for four people.

• Use only metric, Imperial or American measures in a recipe, do not try to combine them.

- Herbs add interest to any salad. Fresh ones are best for chopping and sprinkling over the finished salad as a garnish. But frozen and dried too can be included in the dressing for wonderful variety and flavour.

- Where gherkins are given in the ingredients, they refer to the large bottled variety rather than the small cocktail gherkins.

- There are a number of ready-made, bottled mayonnaises on the market that are quite adequate to substitute for homemade mayonnaise.

- All eggs are size 2 unless otherwise stated.

- Where ingredients call for salt and pepper, for the best flavour use freshly ground black pepper if possible.

- If you need to cook rice for a recipe which calls for it ready cooked, remember it at least trebles on cooking – so 25 g/1 oz/2 tbsp raw rice will give you at least 75 g/3 oz/⅓ cup cooked.

Notes on Preparation and Storage

- Root vegetables should be stored in a cool, dark place.

- All greens (salad, cabbage, etc) keep best in a plastic bag in the drawer at the bottom of the fridge. They must be kept cool and dark. If at all wet when you buy, dry with kitchen paper before storage.

- Do not tear or cut until ready to use or the leaves will start to wilt.

- Ready prepared salads and greens should be used as soon after purchase as possible as they do not keep well.

- Limp lettuce can be revived by plunging in cold water, shaking dry then putting in a covered saucepan or polythene box with a lid in the fridge for a few hours. There are special 'crisp it' boxes available for this purpose too.

- Do not peel button mushrooms, just wash and if necessary chop off the end of the stalk.

- Cook potatoes in the skin and peel when cooked to give better flavour.

- Peel tomatoes easily by searing in the gas flame or dropping briefly into a pan of boiling water.

- When preparing heads of chicory (endive) always cut out a cone shape core from the base. This will prevent the leaves from being too bitter.

- You can replace dried beans with canned ready-cooked varieties for quickness. Make sure you rinse and drain them well before use. A 425 g/15 oz can is equivalent to about 100 g/4 oz dried beans.

STARTERS

In this section I have selected a whole range of recipes which make particularly good starters. Of course, being naturally light, most salads make suitable starters so you will find lots more ideas in other parts of the book. The recipes in Chapter Four, Cooked Salads and Chapter Five, Salads with Fruit are especially suitable.

You might like to try some of the main course recipes at the start of the meal as well. If you do, simply reduce the quantities by about a quarter or a third, depending on how heavy the meal is and the appetites of those eating it.

Alternatively, you could serve together two of the recipes from Chapter Three, A Salad Medley, to make a light starter. Good combinations might be *Raw Mushroom Salad* with *Sweetcorn and Watercress* or *Sprout and Bacon Salad* with *Green Cabbage Vinaigrette with Raisins*.

Many of the recipes in this section would make excellent light lunches. They could also be served with a salad accompaniment such as a green salad or one of the other recipes in the side salad section. Double the quantities to serve four people for lunch.

Artichoke and Bacon Salad

Serves 4

	Metric	Imperial	American
Rashers (slices) rindless streaky bacon	4	4	4
Canned artichoke hearts	8	8	8
Button mushrooms	4	4	4

Recommended dressing:
Oil and vinegar dressing (see page 117)

Grill (broil) the bacon until really crisp. Allow to cool
then break into bite-sized pieces. Chop the artichokes
and mix with the bacon. Pour over the dressing then
toss. Season to taste.

Swedish Beet and Rollmop Salad

Serves 4

	Metric	Imperial	American
Rollmop herrings with onions	2	2	2
Onion, finely chopped (optional)	1	1	1
Cooked beetroot (red beet)	4	4	4
Cucumber	10 cm	4 in	4 in
Gherkins	2	2	2
Salt and pepper			
Recommended dressing:			
Mayonnaise (see page 119)	30-45 ml	2-3 tbsp	2-3 tbsp

Cut off the tails and fins from the rollmops and discard. Dice the flesh. If desired, more finely-chopped onion may be added to the rollmop onion. Dice the beetroot, cucumber and gherkin and mix with the rollmops and onions. Add the mayonnaise and seasoning to taste and serve on a bed of lettuce or endive.

Buckling and Apple Salad

Serves 4

	Metric	Imperial	American
Smoked buckling or any *smoked herring*	2	2	2
Cooked beetroot (red beet)	2	2	2
Cooked potatoes	2	2	2
Eating (dessert) apples	2	2	2
Gherkins	2	2	2

Recommended dressing:

Mayonnaise *(see page 119)*		30-45 ml	2-3 tbsp	2-3 tbsp
Salt and pepper				

Bone and skin the herring then chop the flesh. Dice all other ingredients and mix together with the mayonnaise and seasoning. (This recipe goes well into a salad medley.)

Canadian Crunchy Tuna Salad

Serves 4

	Metric	*Imperial*	*American*
White cabbage	¼	¼	¼
Small green (bell) pepper	1	1	1
Onion	1	1	1
Can tuna, drained	200 g	7 oz	7 oz
Recomended dressing:			
Mayonnaise			
(see page 119)	45 ml	3 tbsp	3 tbsp
Packet potato crisps			
(Saratoga chips)	1	1	1

Slice the cabbage and green pepper very finely. Chop
the onion. Mix together with the flaked tuna and add
mayonnaise. Add the potato crisps just before serving.
Increase the quantities slightly to make an excellent
main course.

Chicken Chop Suey Salad

Serves 4

	Metric	*Imperial*	*American*
Cooked chicken	*225 g*	*8 oz*	*8 oz*
Green (bell) pepper	*½*	*½*	*½*
Carrot	*1*	*1*	*1*
Celery sticks (ribs)	*2*	*2*	*2*
Spring onions (scallions)	*2*	*2*	*2*
Bean sprouts	*100 g*	*4 oz*	*1 cup*

Recommended dressing:
Oriental-style dressing
*   (page 123)*
To garnish:
Lettuce
Tomatoes
Parsley

Chop all the ingredients and mix with the bean sprouts. Toss in Oriental-style dressing. Season to taste. Serve on a bed of lettuce and garnish with sliced tomatoes and parsley.

Cauliflower and Mixed Vegetable Salad

Serves 4

	Metric	Imperial	American
Small cauliflower	½	½	½
Green (bell) pepper	½	½	½
Red (bell) pepper	½	½	½
Button mushrooms	50 g	2 oz	½ cup
Celery sticks (ribs)	2	2	2
Radishes	4	4	4
Cucumber	7.5 cm	3 in	3 in
Grated rind of orange	½	½	½
Grated rind of grapefruit	¼	¼	¼

Recommended dressing:
Oil and vinegar dressing
  (see page 117)
To serve:
Curly endive

Divide the cauliflower into small florets, removing most of the stalk. Chop all other ingredients finely and mix with dressing and grated fruit rind. Serve with curly endive.

Celery, Cheese and Apple Salad

Serves 4

	Metric	Imperial	American
Celery sticks (ribs)	4	4	4
Cheddar cheese	50 g	2 oz	2 oz
Apples	2	2	2
Recommended dressing:			
Mayonnaise (see page 119)	45 ml	3 tbsp	3 tbsp
Salt and pepper			
Parsley to garnish			

Dice all the ingredients and mix together with mayonnaise. Garnish with the finely chopped parsley.

Clam Salad

Serves 4

	Metric	Imperial	American
Can minced clams	225 g	8 oz	8 oz
Spring onions (scallions)	3	3	3
Green (bell) pepper	¼	¼	¼
Celery sticks (ribs)	3	3	3
Recommended dressing:			
Mayonnaise (see page 119)	30 ml	2 tbsp	2 tbsp
Salt and pepper			
To serve:			
Watercress and tomatoes			

Drain the clams and mix with the finely chopped spring onions, green pepper and diced celery. Mix with the mayonnaise and season to taste. Best served with watercress and tomatoes.

Green Bean and Tuna Salad

Serves 4

	Metric	Imperial	American
Fresh or frozen *haricot vert*	*350 g*	*12 oz*	*12 oz*
Shallot *(or ½ small onion)*	*1*	*1*	*1*
Recommended dressing:			
French dressing *(see page 117)*			
Canned tuna, drained	*100 g*	*4 oz*	*1 cup*

Cook the beans in boiling, salted water until just tender – do not overcook. Drain, rinse with cold water and drain again. Slice the onion finely and mix with the beans. Toss in the French dressing and sprinkle with the tuna.

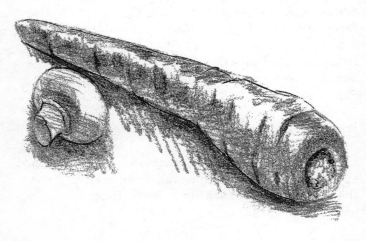

Mediterranean Stuffed Tomatoes

Serves 4

	Metric	Imperial	American
Spring onions (scallions)	4	4	4
Courgette (zucchini)	1	1	1
Cottage cheese	100 g	4 oz	1 cup
Dried basil	2.5 ml	½ tsp	½ tsp
Black olives, stoned (pitted)	4	4	4
Pepper			
Tomatoes	8	8	8

To garnish:
Lettuce leaves

Chop spring onions and grate courgette. Mix with the cheese, basil, olives and a good grinding of pepper. Cut the tops off the tomatoes and scoop out the pulp. Mix half the pulp with the cheese mixture. Pile back into the tomato shells, top with 'lids' if liked and place on a bed of lettuce.

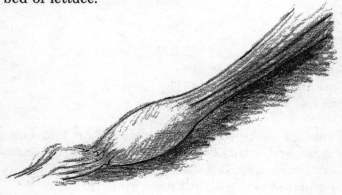

Courgettes Vinaigrette

Serves 4

	Metric	Imperial	American
Large courgettes (zucchini)	4	4	4
Recommended dressing:			
Vinaigrette dressing (see page 118)			
Rosemary			
Small onion	1	1	1

Slice the courgettes thinly then simmer in salted water for 5–7 minutes until just cooked. Drain and toss in vinaigrette sprinkled with rosemary and finely sliced onion. Serve warm or chill before serving.

Leek and Artichoke Salad

Serves 4

	Metric	Imperial	American
Leeks	4	4	4
Canned artichoke hearts	8	8	8
Cooked mussels	16	16	16
Recommended dressing:			
French dressing (see page 117)			
Salt and pepper			

Cook the leeks whole. When cold chop into large chunks and arrange on a plate with the artichoke hearts cut in half. Dot with mussels, pour the dressing over and season with salt and pepper to taste.

Shropska

Serves 4

	Metric	Imperial	American
Celery sticks (ribs)	3	3	3
Green (bell) pepper	1	1	1
Small onion	1	1	1
Cucumber	10 cm	4 in	4 in
Firm tomatoes	4	4	4
Cheese – Cheddar, Lancashire or Cheshire, grated	100 g	4 oz	1 cup
Juice of lemon	1	1	1
Freshly chopped marjoram			

Coarsely chop all the ingredients except the cheese and toss in the lemon juice. Place in individual bowls and sprinkle with the grated cheese and marjoram. Try varying the herbs to give different flavours to the salad, e.g. basil, rosemary, thyme. This recipe makes an excellent main course for slimmers.

Marinated Fish Salad

Serves 4

	Metric	Imperial	American
Fresh white fish	225 g	8 oz	8 oz
Juice of lemons or limes	3	3	3
Small onions	2	2	2
Green (bell) pepper	1	1	1
Salt and pepper			

Skin the fish and remove any bones. Cut into small cubes and cover with lemon or lime juice. Slice the onions finely and chop the pepper. Place on top of the fish but steeped in the lemon juice. Sprinkle with salt and pepper. Chill for at least 4 hours (it can be left overnight). Turn occasionally in the marinade.

Serve on its own on a bed of lettuce or endive. Or mix with tomato and cucumber, or with melon and grapes before serving.

Note: As the fish is not cooked, just marinated until opaque, it must be very fresh indeed.

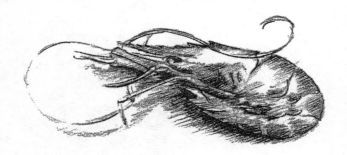

Spicy Prawn Salad

Serves 6

	Metric	Imperial	American
Soured (dairy sour) cream	150 ml	¼ pt	⅔ cup
Ready-made tomato			
spaghetti sauce	45 ml	3 tbsp	3 tbsp
Lemon juice	5 ml	1 tsp	1 tsp
Grated onion	2.5 ml	½ tsp	½ tsp
Horseradish cream	5 ml	1 tsp	1 tsp
Worcestershire sauce	2.5 ml	½ tsp	½ tsp
Few drops Tabasco sauce			
Salt and pepper			
Peeled prawns (shrimp)	225-350 g	8-12 oz	8-12 oz

To garnish:
Shredded lettuce
Lemon wedges
Paprika

Mix all the ingredients except prawns together. Pile the seafood on individual beds of lettuce on serving plates. Spoon the sauce over and garnish with lemon wedges. Dust with a little paprika before serving.

This recipe will serve up to six people as a starter.

Mint and Cucumber Fish Salad

Serves 4

	Metric	Imperial	American
Cooked cod	350 g	12 oz	12 oz
Cucumber	10 cm	4 in	4 in
Chopped fresh parsley	5 ml	2 tsp	2 tsp
Chopped fresh mint	5 ml	2 tsp	2 tsp
Recommended dressing:			
French dressing			
(see page 117)			
Salt and pepper			
To garnish:			
Peeled prawns (shrimp)	50 g	2 oz	½ cup
Lemon wedges			
To serve:			
Brown bread and butter			

Remove the skin and bones from the fish and flake coarsely. Dice the cucumber and add to the fish. Sprinkle on the freshly chopped herbs and toss in the dressing, being careful not to break up the fish. Place on individual plates and garnish with peeled prawns and lemon wedges. Serve with brown bread and butter. Using 450 g/1 lb of fish and a little more cucumber, this recipe makes a good main course dish.

Salad Kebabs with Savoury Rice

Serves 4

	Metric	*Imperial*	*American*
Cooked savoury rice per person (see page 79)	*30 ml*	*2 tbsp*	*2 tbsp*
Kebabs per person (see below)	*3*	*3*	*3*

To garnish:
Cress

Place the savoury rice onto the plates and arrange three kebabs on top of each plate. Garnish with cress.

The kebabs can be made up of any available ingredients, leftovers, etc. Some ideas are set out below. (Use cocktail sticks [toothpicks] for skewers.)

1. Pineapple chunks
   Ham cubes
   Cheese cubes
   Tomato wedges

2. Frankfurter pieces
   Green (bell) pepper diced
   White grapes
   Baby cooked potatoes

3. Button mushrooms
   Crispy grilled (broiled) bacon, diced
   Cheese cubes
   Diced cucumber

4. Green (bell) pepper diced
   Chicken cubes
   Tomato wedges
   Sausage pieces

Use smoked oysters or mussels or other fish. Radishes, diced carrots and cocktail onions will lend other flavours and colour to the kebabs.

Smoked Clam Salad

Serves 4

	Metric	*Imperial*	*American*
Long-grain rice	50	2 oz	¼ cup
Green (bell) pepper	¼	¼	¼
Large mushrooms	2	2	2
Can sweetcorn (corn)	200 g	7 oz	7 oz
Flaked almonds	25 g	1 oz	¼ cup
Can smoked clams, drained	105 g	4¼ oz	4¼ oz
Lemon juice			
Salt and pepper			

To garnish:
Lettuce
Lemon wedges

Cook the rice and drain. When cold, mix with the finely chopped green pepper and mushrooms. Add drained sweetcorn and almonds. Mix in smoked clams and a little lemon juice. Season to taste. Pile on a bed of lettuce and garnish with wedges of lemon.

Note: Substitute smoked mussels for clams if you prefer.

Stuffed Tomatoes

Serves 4

	Metric	*Imperial*	*American*
Tomatoes	8	8	8
Cooked long-grain rice	30 ml	2 tbsp	2 tbsp
Button mushrooms	4	4	4
Can sardines, drained	120 g	5 oz	5 oz
Recommended dressing:			
Mayonnaise (see page 119)	15 ml	1 tbsp	1 tbsp
Salt and pepper			
To garnish:			
Lettuce			
Watercress			

Remove the tops of the tomatoes and put to one side. Scoop out the pulp and mix with the rice and the finely chopped mushrooms. Mash the sardines with the mayonnaise and add to the rice mixture. Season to taste. Stuff the tomatoes with the mixture and pile up high. Top with the slices from the top of the tomatoes. As an alternative, try prawns (shrimp) and finely chopped red (bell) pepper in place of sardines and mushrooms.

Italian Mozzarella and Tomato Salad

Serves 4

	Metric	*Imperial*	*American*
Beef tomatoes	2	2	2
Whole Mozzarella cheese	2	2	2

To garnish:
Fresh basil
Black olives
Balsamic vinegar
Salt and pepper

Slice the tomatoes fairly thickly and arrange on the plate. Slice the Mozzarella cheese and layer on top of the tomato. Garnish with roughly torn, fresh basil leaves and a few black olives. Drizzle over balsamic vinegar and season to taste. Alternatively, use Honeyed Italian-style dressing (see page 122).

Herby Cheese and Avocado Salad

Serves 4

	Metric	*Imperial*	*American*
Ripe avocados	2	2	2
Lemon juice			
Garlic and herb			
soft cheese	80 g	3¼ oz	3¼ oz
Stuffed olives, sliced	15 ml	1 tbsp	1 tbsp
Green, red or yellow			
(bell) pepper	½	½	½
Milk			

Halve the avocados, remove stones (pits) and brush surfaces with lemon juice to prevent discolouring. Mash cheese with olives. Finely chop the pepper and mix in with a little milk if necessary to soften mixture slightly. Pile into cavities in avocados and serve in avocado dishes.

Alternatively, serve on small plates on a bed of lettuce.

MAIN COURSES AND LIGHT MEALS

Salads make nourishing main courses and light meals. The recipes in this section are designed to be served on their own, possibly with a garnish of lettuce, watercress and tomato. Rice and potatoes should be cooked a little less than for a hot dish. They must be firm, never soft or soggy. The amount of dressing given in the recipes for adding to the salads can be varied according to taste.

For other main course ideas, try enlarged starter recipes or three or four of the recipes from the salad medley section.

Plate Salads

For an interesting cheese salad try arranging the following ingredients in a random manner on individual plates: a little lettuce (of any variety), watercress, chicory (endive), fennel leaves, parsley, spring onion (scallion) and radishes. Grate or slice a variety of cheeses of your choice and pile them in the centre of the plate. Alternatively, try ham salad with chopped endive, sliced green (bell) peppers, cucumber and spring onions arranged at one side of the plate and asparagus rolled up in ham on the other side.

Try experimenting with the very many different vegetable and salad ingredients available with the season and invent your own mixtures including Chinese leaves, fennel, chicory, endive, spring greens, spinach, cabbage, beans and peas. The addition of fresh herbs to salads adds variety, so try parsley, mint, rosemary, thyme, borage, sorrel, basil, dandelion, nasturtium leaves and marigold petals.

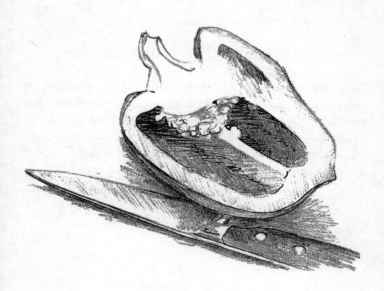

Austrian Salad

Serves 4

	Metric	*Imperial*	*American*
Lettuce heart	1	1	1
Firm cheese	100 g	4 oz	4 oz
Eating (dessert) apples	3	3	3
Gherkins	4	4	4
Large celery sticks (ribs)	6	6	6
Can of cocktail sausages (20)			
Tomatoes	4	4	4

Recommended dressing:
Oil and vinegar dressing
  (see page 117)
To garnish:
Cress or watercress
Hard-boiled
  (hard-cooked) eggs

Tear the lettuce into pieces and place in the base of four dishes. Dice the cheese, apples, gherkins and celery and mix with the sliced sausages and tomatoes. Toss in dressing and serve on the lettuce bed garnished with watercress or cress and the hard-boiled eggs, coarsely chopped.

American Luncheon Salad

Serves 4

	Metric	Imperial	American
Cooked ham	225 g	8 oz	8 oz
Grated cheese	100 g	4 oz	1 cup
Celery sticks (ribs)	3	3	3
Green (bell) pepper	½	½	½
Spring onions (scallions)	3	3	3
Radishes	4	4	4

Recommended dressing:
Oil and lemon dressing
  (see page 117)
To garnish:
Lettuce
Tomato
Garlic croûtons

Cube the ham and mix with the cheese. Add the finely chopped celery, green pepper, spring onions and radishes. Toss in the dressing and serve on a bed of lettuce. Garnish with wedges of tomato and sprinkle with garlic croûtons.

Note: You can buy garlic croûtons ready made, or make your own: Simply fry (sauté) small cubes of day-old bread in a little oil with a crushed clove of garlic added. Or fry plain and toss in garlic salt. Drain on kitchen paper and cool before serving.

Danish Chef's Salad

Serves 4

	Metric	Imperial	American
Cos (Romaine) lettuce	½	½	½
Bunch radishes	1	1	1
Cucumber	¼	¼	¼
Onion	1	1	1
Cooked ham, shredded	225 g	8 oz	1 cup
Danish blue cheese, cubed	10 g	4 oz	1 cup
Salt and pepper			

Recommended dressing:
*Vinaigrette dressing
  (see page 118)*

Slice the lettuce, radishes, cucumber and onion and
layer with the cubed cheese and shredded ham.
Season to taste and toss lightly with the dressing just
before serving.

Chicken and Almond Salad

Serves 4

	Metric	*Imperial*	*American*
Green (bell) pepper	½	½	½
Red (bell) pepper	½	½	½
Heads of small chicory (endive)	2	2	2
Small can of pineapple chunks	220 g	8 oz	8 oz
Cooked chicken, diced	350 g	12 oz	1½ cups
Toasted split almonds	50 g	2 oz	½ cup
Recommended dressing:			
Mayonnaise (see page 119)	45 ml	3 tbsp	3 tbsp
Salt and pepper			

Chop the peppers, chicory and pineapple. Mix with the
chicken and almonds and mix in mayonnaise. Season
to taste.

Chicken and Avocado Salad

Serves 4

	Metric	*Imperial*	*American*
Large ripe avocado	1	1	1
Juice of orange	1	1	1
Cooked chicken	450 g	1 lb	1 lb
Celery sticks (ribs)	2	2	2
Grapes	100 g	4 oz	1 cup
Salt and pepper			

To garnish:
Endive
Tomato
Chopped fresh parsley

Peel and stone (pit) the avocado. Cut into small chunks and put straight in the orange juice to avoid discolouration. Dice the chicken and celery and mix with the avocado. Add halved and de-seeded (pitted) grapes and season to taste. Serve on a bed of endive and garnish with tomato and parsley.

Mixed Greek Salad

Serves 4

	Metric	Imperial	American
Cucumber	1	1	1
Onion	1	1	1
Tomatoes	2	2	2
Feta cheese	100 g	4 oz	4 oz
Hard-boiled (hard-cooked) egg	1	1	1
Black olives, stoned (pitted)	8	8	8
Fresh chopped or dried oregano			
Recommended dressing:			
Oil and vinegar dressing (see page 117)	250 ml	8 fl oz	1 cup
Salt and pepper			

Slice the cucumber and onion. Cut the tomatoes into wedges and cube the Feta cheese. Mix all of these ingredients together. Arrange the egg, cut into wedges, and the olives on top. Sprinkle with a little fresh chopped or dried oregano. Just before serving, spoon the dressing over the salad and toss gently. Season to taste.

Indian Nutty Chicken Salad

Serves 4

	Metric	Imperial	American
Cooked potatoes	4	4	4
Juice of lime	½	½	½
Cooked chicken, diced	450 g	1 lb	2 cups
Green (bell) pepper	1	1	1
Green chilli (chili)	1	1	1
Cabbage, shredded	45 ml	3 tbsp	3 tbsp
Mayonnaise	60 ml	4 tbsp	4 tbsp
Walnut halves	175 g	6 oz	1½ cups
Salt and pepper			
To garnish:			
Lettuce leaves	5-6	5-6	5-6

Cube the potatoes and toss in the lime juice. Stir in the diced chicken. Slice the pepper into strips, de-seed and chop the chilli and add to the chicken along with all the remaining ingredients. Pile on a bed of lettuce and serve.

Crunchy Egg Salad

Serves 4

	Metric	*Imperial*	*American*
Chinese leaves	*12*	*12*	*12*
Hard-boiled (hard-cooked) eggs	*4*	*4*	*4*
Firm cheese	*175 g*	*6 oz*	*6 oz*
Small green (bell) pepper	*1*	*1*	*1*
Cucumber	*¼*	*¼*	*¼*
Recommended dressing:			
Mayonnaise (see page 119)	*60 ml*	*4 tbsp*	*4 tbsp*
Lemon juice or vinegar			
Salt and pepper			
To garnish:			
Tomatoes or watercress			
Chopped fresh parsley			

Coarsely chop all the ingredients and combine with mayonnaise and vinegar. Season with salt and pepper. Garnish with tomatoes or watercress as available. Sprinkle with fresh chopped parsley. Chicory (endive) can be substituted for Chinese leaves.

Mixed Meat Salad

Serves 4

Equal quantities of:
Cooked chicken, diced
Cooked ham, diced
Cooked beef or pork, diced
Flavoured mayonnaise to mix (see page 119)
Salt and pepper
To garnish:
Lettuce, tomato and watercress

Mix the diced meats with mayonnaise and seasonings.
Chill for 30 minutes and then serve, piled up on a bed
of lettuce, garnished with tomato and watercress.

For an unusual variation, serve a:

Mixed Meat Platter
Allow 3-4 slices of different continental meats and
sausages per person. Arrange attractively on a serving
plate with a small dish of flavoured mayonnaise in the
centre. Garnish with watercress and serve with any
vegetable salads of your choice.

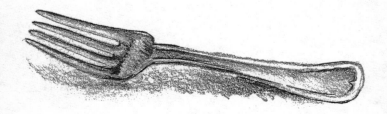

Curried Ham and Yoghurt Salad

Serves 4

	Metric	Imperial	American
Eating (dessert) apple	*1*	*1*	*1*
Juice of lemon	*1*	*1*	*1*
Ham	*225 g*	*8 oz*	*8 oz*
Mushrooms	*100 g*	*4 oz*	*1 cup*
Raisins	*15 ml*	*1 tbsp*	*1 tbsp*
Natural (plain) yoghurt	*150 ml*	*¼ pt*	*⅔ cup*
Curry powder	*5 ml*	*1 tsp*	*1 tsp*

To garnish:
Chopped fresh parsley
To serve:
Chutney

Core and chop the apple and sprinkle with lemon juice. Dice the ham and mushrooms and add with the raisins to the apple and lemon juice mixture. Mix the yoghurt and curry powder and pour over the ham mixture. Sprinkle with chopped parsley and serve with chutney.

Macaroni Salad

Serves 4

	Metric	*Imperial*	*American*
Macaroni	*100 g*	*4 oz*	*1 cup*
Hard-boiled *(hard-cooked) eggs*	*3*	*3*	*3*
Canned chopped ham *with pork*	*200 g*	*7 oz*	*7 oz*
Green (bell) pepper	*½*	*½*	*½*
Gherkin	*1*	*1*	*1*
Recommended dressing:			
Mayonnaise *(see page 119)*	*45 ml*	*3 tbsp*	*3 tbsp*

To garnish:
Chopped fresh parsley
Lettuce
Tomato
Watercress

Cook the macaroni in plenty of boiling, salted water until just tender. Drain, rinse with cold water and drain again. Chop the eggs, meat, green pepper and gherkin and mix with the macaroni and mayonnaise. Sprinkle with freshly chopped parsley and pile on a bed of lettuce, garnished with tomato or watercress. Try prawns (shrimp) instead of chopped ham with pork for a different flavour.

Hawaiian Turkey

Serves 4

	Metric	Imperial	American
Fresh pineapples	2	2	2
Cooked turkey meat	350 g	12 oz	12 oz
White grapes	75 g	3 oz	¾ cup
Red (bell) pepper	1	1	1
Cashew nuts	50 g	2 oz	½ cup
Soured (dairy sour) cream	150 ml	¼ pt	⅔ cup
Soft brown sugar	25 g	1 oz	2 tbsp
Salt and pepper			

Cut pineapples in half. Scoop out most of the flesh and dice. Place in a bowl. Dice turkey and add with the halved and seeded (pitted) grapes, finely diced pepper and cashews. Mix sugar with soured cream and a little salt and pepper. Pour over, toss and then pile mixture back into pineapple skins. Chill, if time, before serving.

Tropical Ham Salad

Serves 4

	Metric	*Imperial*	*American*
Cooked ham	225 g	8 oz	8 oz
Canned grapefruit segments	420 g	15 oz	15 oz
Canned mandarin oranges	300 g	11 oz	11 oz
Coconut flakes	25 g	1 oz	¼ cup
Ripe avocado	1	1	1
Recommended dressing:			
Soured cream dressing (see page 121)			
Horseradish cream	5 ml	1 tsp	1 tsp
To garnish:			
Lettuce			
Chopped fresh parsley			

Dice the ham. Drain the canned fruits. Mix in a bowl with the coconut flakes. Peel the avocado, remove the stone (pit) and cut into dice. Toss in a little of the grapefruit juice to prevent discolouring. Add to the bowl. Mix the soured cream dressing with horseradish cream. Pour over mixture in bowl and lightly toss. Pile onto a bed of lettuce and garnish with chopped parsley.

Dutch Hussar Salad

Serves 4

	Metric	Imperial	American
Cooked chicken (or pork or lamb)	350 g	12 oz	12 oz
Hard-boiled (hard-cooked) eggs	2	2	2
Eating (dessert) apple	1	1	1
Large boiled potatoes	2	2	2
Pickled onions	2	2	2
Salt and pepper			

Recommended dressing:

Mayonnaise (see page 119)	90 ml	6 tbsp	6 tbsp

To garnish:
Pimiento strips
A few whole prawns (shrimp)
Capers

Dice all the ingredients and mix with 30 ml/2 tbsp of the mayonnaise. Season. The salad should be fairly solid. Place on a bed of lettuce and spread a thick layer of mayonnaise on the top. Decorate with pimiento strips, a few whole prawns and capers.

Creole Potato Salad

Serves 4

	Metric	Imperial	American
Potatoes	*450 g*	*1 lb*	*1 lb*
Prawns (shrimp)	*100 g*	*4 oz*	*1 cup*
Hard-boiled (hard-cooked) *eggs, chopped*	*4*	*4*	*4*
Small green (bell) *pepper, chopped*	*1*	*1*	*1*
Salt and pepper			
Recommended dressing:			
French dressing *(see page 117)*	*45 ml*	*3 tbsp*	*3 tbsp*

Cook the potatoes, dice and mix with the prawns while still warm. Season. Mix in the chopped eggs and green pepper and dressing. Canned pimientos may be used for a change or if green peppers are not available.

Mushroom and Egg Salad

Serves 4

	Metric	Imperial	American
Cooked potatoes	*450 g*	*1 lb*	*1 lb*
Mushrooms	*175 g*	*6 oz*	*6 oz*
Celery sticks (ribs)	*4*	*4*	*4*
Bunch watercress	*1*	*1*	*1*
Recommended dressing:			
French cream dressing *(see page 120)*			
Sliced hard-boiled *(hard-cooked) eggs*	*4*	*4*	*4*
Parsley to garnish			

Chop the potatoes, mushrooms and celery and mix with the watercress and mayonnaise. Season to taste. Pile on a bed of lettuce and top with sliced egg. Garnish with chopped fresh parsley.

Madrid Salad

Serves 4

	Metric	Imperial	American
Hard-boiled (hard-cooked) eggs	8	8	8
Radicchio	1	1	1
Small iceberg lettuce	1	1	1
Large onion	1	1	1
Tomatoes	2	2	2
Goat's cheese	225 g	8 oz	8 oz
Feta cheese	175 g	6 oz	6 oz
Black olives, stoned (pitted)	100 g	4 oz	1 cup
Pickled capers	30 ml	2 tbsp	2 tbsp
Salt and pepper			

Recommended dressing:
*Garlic Dressing
(see page 121)*

Cut the hard-boiled eggs into wedges. Shred the radicchio and the lettuce. Slice the onion and dice the tomatoes. Break the cheeses into bite-sized pieces and toss all the remaining ingredients together. Serve with the Garlic Dressing.

Bacon, Egg and Cheese Salad

Serves 4

	Metric	*Imperial*	*American*
Hard-boiled (hard-cooked) eggs	4	4	4
Streaky bacon rashers (slices)	8	8	8
Head lettuce	1	1	1
Spring onions (scallions)	4	4	4
Slice bread, toasted	1	1	1
Garlic clove, halved	1	1	1
Cottage cheese	225 g	8 oz	2 cups

Recommended dressing:
*French dressing
   (see page 117)*

Peel then roughly chop the eggs. Grill (broil) the bacon until crisp, drain on kitchen paper. Roughly crumble. Tear lettuce into bite-sized pieces. Chop the spring onions. Rub toast on both sides with the garlic. Cut into small dice and place in a salad bowl. Add lettuce and sprinkle with onions. Cover and chill. When ready to serve, toss salad in a bowl with French dressing. Spoon cottage cheese over and sprinkle on the bacon and eggs.

Tuna and Pasta Salad

Serves 4

	Metric	Imperial	American
Pasta shells	100 g	4 oz	1 cup
Red skinned apples	2	2	2
Celery sticks (ribs)	2	2	2
Green (bell) pepper	½	½	½
Canned tuna	200 g	7 oz	7 oz

Recommended dressing:

Oil and vinegar dressing (see page 117)	30 ml	2 tbsp	2 tbsp

Salt and pepper

To garnish:

Tomato wedges

To serve:

Lettuce or endive

Cook the pasta shells in plenty of boiling, salted water. Drain, rinse with cold water and drain again. Chop the apples, celery and green pepper and flake the drained tuna. Mix all ingredients together and toss in the dressing (adding a little more if necessary). Season to taste. Serve on a bed of lettuce or curly endive. Garnish with tomato wedges.

Smoked Mackerel Salad

Serves 4

	Metric	Imperial	American
Long-grain rice	75 g	3 oz	⅓ cup
Smoked mackerel fillets	2	2	2
Tomatoes	2	2	2
Cucumber	5 cm	2 in	2 in
Mushrooms	4	4	4
Green (bell) pepper	½	½	½
Salt and pepper			

Recommended dressing:
*Oil and vinegar dressing
  (see page 117)*

Cook the rice in plenty of boiling, salted water until tender. Drain, rinse with cold water and drain again. Skin the mackerel, remove the bones and flake. Dice the tomato, cucumber, mushrooms and green pepper. Mix all ingredients together. Season to taste and moisten with oil and vinegar dressing.

Savoury Rice Cake

Serves 4

	Metric	Imperial	American
Long-grain rice	75 g	3 oz	⅓ cup
*Hard-boiled
(hard-cooked) eggs*	4	4	4
Rollmop herrings	2	2	2
Beetroot (red beet)	2	2	2
Gherkins	4	4	4
Soured (dairy sour) cream	30 ml	2 tbsp	2 tbsp
Salt and pepper			

Cook the rice in boiling, salted water until tender. Drain, rinse with cold water and drain again. Chop the eggs and herrings and cube the beetroot and gherkins. Mix all the ingredients together with a little soured cream and season to taste. Rinse your hands with cold water and shape the mixture into a block on a board also rinsed under the cold tap, or press into a ring or pudding mould (mold). Chill for 1 hour before turning out and serving.

Indonesian-style Rice Salad

Serves 4

	Metric	Imperial	American
Long-grain rice	175 g	6 oz	¾ cup
Salt			
Bean sprouts	50 g	2 oz	1 cup
Spring onions (scallions)	4	4	4
Toasted flaked almonds	50 g	2 oz	½ cup
Curry Mayonnaise (see page 119)	60 ml	4 tbsp	4 tbsp
Mango chutney	15 ml	1 tbsp	1 tbsp
Natural (plain) yoghurt	45 ml	3 tbsp	3 tbsp
Soy sauce	15 ml	1 tbsp	1 tbsp

Cook the rice in plenty of boiling, salted water. Drain, rinse with cold water and drain again. Add bean sprouts, finely chopped spring onions and almonds. Mix the curry mayonnaise with the chutney, yoghurt and Soy sauce. Add to the rice mixture and toss well.

Cheesey Apricot Rice Ring

Serves 4

	Metric	*Imperial*	*American*
Long-grain rice	*175 g*	*6 oz*	*¾ cup*
Peas	*50 g*	*2 oz*	*⅓ cup*
Currants	*50 g*	*2 oz*	*⅓ cup*
Flaked almonds	*25 g*	*1 oz*	*¼ cup*
Recommended dressing:			
Oil and vinegar dressing (see page 117)			
Cheddar cheese	*100 g*	*4 oz*	*4 oz*
Dried ready-to-eat apricots	*100 g*	*4 oz*	*⅔ cup*
Natural (plain) yoghurt	*45 ml*	*3 tbsp*	*3 tbsp*
Salt and pepper			
To garnish:			
Chopped (snipped) chives			

Cook the rice in plenty of boiling, salted water until just tender. Add peas for last 5 minutes. Drain, rinse with cold water and then drain again. Stir in the currants, almonds and dressing. Press into a 1.2 l/2 pt/ 5 cup ring mould (mold) and chill. Meanwhile, dice the cheese. Roughly cut up apricots. Mix with yoghurt and a little salt and pepper. Turn out rice ring onto a serving plate. Pile cheese mixture in the centre and garnish with chopped chives.

English Roast Beef Salad

Serves 4

	Metric	*Imperial*	*American*
Carrots	2	2	2
New potatoes	*350 g*	*12 oz*	*12 oz*
Peas	*100 g*	*4 oz*	*1 cup*
Mayonnaise			
(see page 119)	*45 ml*	*3 tbsp*	*3 tbsp*
Lemon juice	*5 ml*	*1 tsp*	*1 tsp*
Salt and pepper			
Lettuce leaves			
Roast beef slices	8	8	8
Horseradish cream			

To garnish:
Parsley sprigs
Tomato wedges

Scrape and dice carrots and potatoes and cook in boiling, salted water until just tender. Add peas for last few minutes cooking. Drain, rinse with cold water and drain again. Mix the mayonnaise with the lemon juice, add to vegetables and toss, seasoning to taste. Pile onto a bed of lettuce. Spread beef slices thinly with horseradish cream. Roll up and arrange on top of the vegetables. Garnish with parsley sprigs and tomato wedges.

Thai Beef Salad

Serves 4

	Metric	Imperial	American
Cooked beef	450 g	1 lb	1 lb
Transparent noodles	25 g	1 oz	¼ cup
Onion	1	1	1
Stick lemon grass	1	1	1
Cucumber	½	½	½
Spring onions (scallions)	3	3	3
Whole red chilli (chili)	1	1	1
Lime juice	15 ml	1 tbsp	1 tbsp
Thai fish sauce (or anchovy essence (extract))	15 ml	1 tbsp	1 tbsp
Chopped fresh mint	30 ml	2 tbsp	2 tbsp

Soak the noodles in hot water for about 10 minutes.
Drain and cut into pieces. Slice the beef into strips,
slice the onion, lemon grass and cucumber and chop
the spring onions and de-seeded chilli. Mix all of the
ingredients with the lime juice, fish sauce and mint.
Toss with the noodles and chill before serving.

Taco Salad

Serves 4

	Metric	Imperial	American
Minced (ground) beef	225 g	8 oz	1 cup
Chilli (chili) powder	5 ml	1 tsp	1 tsp
Ground cumin	2.5 ml	½ tsp	½ tsp
Salt	1.5 ml	¼ tsp	¼ tsp
Iceberg lettuce	½	½	½
Tortilla chips	100 g	4 oz	2 cups
Canned mixed vegetables, drained	425 g	15 oz	15 oz
Tomato	1	1	1
Edam cheese	225 g	8 oz	8 oz
Spring onions (scallions)	4	4	4
Mild chilli (chili) sauce	100 g	4 oz	½ cup
Soured (dairy sour) cream	150 ml	¼ pt	⅔ cup

Brown the beef in a frying pan (skillet) with the spices and salt. Stir until the meat is brown and crumbly. Leave to cool. Tear the lettuce into small pieces. Mix with the tortilla chips in a large salad bowl. Pile the mixed vegetables in the centre. Surround with the beef and the chopped tomato. Dice cheese and scatter around with the chopped spring onions. Blend the mild chilli sauce with the soured cream and spoon over at the table.

A SALAD MEDLEY

This is a selection of salad recipes which, if served in twos, make good starters or in threes, fours or fives make an exciting main course. Make up your own combinations of salads so as to get a variety of ingredients, colours and textures.

Here are eight suggested selections taken from this and other chapters to start you off.

1. Beet and Cheese Salad
   Raw Artichoke Salad
   Brussels Sprouts with Nuts
   Carrot and Raisin Salad

2. Lemon Fennel Salad
   Carrot and Orange.Salad
   Cucumber, Potato and Herring Salad
   Mushrooms in Cream Cheese

3. Watercress and Pimiento Salad
   Raw Beetroot Salad
   Cheese and Mushroom Salad
   Potato and Bacon Salad

4. Chinese Leaves with Beetroot
   Haricot Bean Salad
   Avocado and Tomato Salad
   Cheese-stuffed Peaches

5. Buckling and Apple Salad
   Bean Sprout and Mushroom Salad
   Carrot and Orange Salad
   Courgettes Vinaigrette

6. Thai Salad
   Prawn and Mushroom Salad
   Bacon and Green Salad
   Savoury Rice

7. Chinese Spinach Salad
   Mushroom and Cream Cheese Salad
   Mandarin Ham Salad
   Haricot Verts Vinaigrette

8. Green Cabbage Vinaigrette
   Red and Green Pepper Salad
   Sweetcorn and Watercress Salad
   Chicken with Melon

Bean Sprout Salad

Serves 4

	Metric	Imperial	American
Bean sprouts	100 g	4 oz	1 cup
Green (bell) pepper	½	½	½
Large celery sticks (ribs)	2	2	2
Flaked almonds	30 ml	2 tbsp	2 tbsp
Pinch of thyme			
Recommended dressing:			
Vinaigrette dressing			
(see page 118)	30 ml	2 tbsp	2 tbsp

Finely slice the green pepper and celery. Toss all ingredients together with the vinaigrette and serve.

Bean Sprout and Mushroom Salad

Serves 4

	Metric	Imperial	American
Button mushrooms, sliced	100 g	4 oz	1 cup
Bean sprouts	100 g	4 oz	1 cup
Gherkins, sliced	2	2	2
Recommended dressing:			
French dressing			
(see page 117)	30 ml	2 tbsp	2 tbsp
Soy sauce	5 ml	1 tsp	1 tsp
Black pepper			

Mix the mushrooms with the bean sprouts and sliced gherkins. Toss in the French dressing and sprinkle with Soy sauce and black pepper. This makes a good light starter on its own or with one other salad.

Beet and Cheese Salad

Serves 4

	Metric	Imperial	American
Beetroot (red beet), cooked and peeled	2	2	2
Cheddar cheese	100 g	4 oz	4 oz
Green (bell) pepper	1	1	1
Celery sticks (ribs)	4	4	4
Recommended dressing:			
Mayonnaise (see page 119)	30 ml	2 tbsp	2 tbsp
Salt and pepper			

Dice the beetroot and cheese and finely chop the green pepper and celery. Mix together with the mayonnaise and season to taste.

Brussels Sprouts with Nuts

Serves 4

	Metric	Imperial	American
Cooked shelled chestnuts or walnuts	8	8	8
Brussels sprouts	8	8	8
Small eating (dessert) apple	1	1	1
Chopped fresh parsley	5 ml	1 tsp	1 tsp
Recommended dressing:			
Cheese Mayonnaise (see page 119)	30 ml	2 tbsp	2 tbsp

Finely chop the cooked shelled chestnuts or walnuts. Next finely chop the sprouts, apple and parsley and mix all ingredients thoroughly together with the cheese mayonnaise.

Bacon Green Salad

Serves 4

	Metric	Imperial	American
Spring greens or spinach leaves per person	1-2	1-2	1-2
Rasher (slice) of streaky bacon per person	1	1	1
Recommended dressing:			
Sherry dressing (see page 118)	15 ml	1 tbsp	1 tbsp

Wash and shred the greens as finely as possible. Grill (broil) the bacon until really crisp, and allow to cool. Chop finely. Sprinkle over the cabbage and toss in the dressing. Season if liked.

Carrot and Orange Salad

Serves 4

	Metric	Imperial	American
Carrots, grated	2	2	2
Orange	1	1	1
Salt and pepper			
Olive oil (optional)			

Squeeze the juice from the orange and pour over the grated carrots. Sprinkle with the salt and pepper. The carrots can be grated coarsely or finely according to taste. Try with lemon juice for a sharper taste. Add a drizzle of olive oil if liked.

Carrot and Raisin Salad

Serves 4

	Metric	*Imperial*	*American*
Good size carrots	2	2	2
Olive oil	*15 ml*	*1 tbsp*	*1 tbsp*
Raisins	*15 ml*	*1 tbsp*	*1 tbsp*
Juice of lemon	½	½	½
Pepper			

Grate the carrots, coarsely or finely according to taste, mix with the oil to prevent them from discolouring. Stir in the raisins and pour over the lemon juice. Mix throughly and sprinkle with pepper.

Cheese and Mushroom Salad

Serves 4

	Metric	*Imperial*	*American*
Mushrooms	*100 g*	*4 oz*	*4 oz*
Small green (bell) pepper	1	1	1
Shallot	1	1	1
Hard cheese, grated	*100 g*	*4 oz*	*1 cup*
Recommended dressing:			
Mayonnaise			
(see page 119)	*30 ml*	*2 tbsp*	*2 tbsp*

Chop the mushrooms, pepper and shallot. Then mix all the ingredients together thoroughly with the mayonnaise.

Green Cabbage Vinaigrette with Raisins

	Metric	Imperial	American
Per person:			
Large leaf of spring greens/			
hearted cabbage	1	1	1
Recommended dressing:			
Vinaigrette dressing			
(see page 118)	15 ml	1 tbsp	1 tbsp
Raisins	5 ml	1 tsp	1 tsp
Pepper			

Wash and shred the spring greens/cabbage as finely as possible. Toss in the dressing and sprinkle with the raisins and pepper.

Chinese Leaves with Beetroot

Serves 4

	Metric	Imperial	American
Good sized cooked			
beetroot (red beet)	2	2	2
Chinese leaves	6	6	6
Recommended dressing:			
Yoghurt dressing			
(see page 121)	30 ml	2 tbsp	2 tbsp
Salt and pepper			
To garnish:			
Fresh chopped thyme			

Dice the beetroot and chop the Chinese leaves. Mix together with the yoghurt dressing and season. Serve immediately sprinkled with fresh chopped thyme. Chicory (endive) may be used instead of Chinese leaves.

Lemon Fennel Salad

Serves 4

	Metric	Imperial	American
Lemon	1	1	1
Olive oil	30 ml	2 tbsp	2 tbsp
Natural (plain) yoghurt	30 ml	2 tbsp	2 tbsp
Sugar	10 ml	2 tsp	2 tsp
Salt and pepper			
Large fennel bulb	1	1	1
To garnish:			
Black olives, stoned (pitted)	6	6	6

Cut the lemon in half. Cut one half into thick slices and trim away the peel. Peel the other half, purée the flesh with the juice along with the oil, yoghurt, sugar and seasoning. Blend until thick. Slice the fennel and toss in the dressing. Garnish with the olives.

Mushrooms with Cream Cheese

Serves 4

	Metric	Imperial	American
Mushrooms, chopped	100 g	4 oz	1 cup
Cream cheese	100 g	4 oz	½ cup
Little milk			
Salt and pepper			
To garnish:			
Fresh chopped (snipped) chives			

Mix the mushrooms with the cream cheese. Add a little milk if the mixture seems too stiff, but add the minimum as the juice comes out of the mushrooms if left to stand. Season to taste and garnish with chopped chives.

Potato and Bacon Salad

Serves 4

	Metric	Imperial	American
Bacon rashers (slices)	4	4	4
Hard cheese, sliced	75 g	3 oz	⅓ cup
Gherkins	2	2	2
Small onion or shallot	1	1	1
Chopped fresh parsley	5 ml	1 tsp	1 tsp
Cooked potatoes	350 g	12 oz	12 oz

Recommended dressing:

*Oil and vinegar dressing
  (see page 117)*

Grill (broil) the bacon until crisp. Allow to cool and chop. Mix the cheese with the finely chopped gherkins, onion and parsley. Mix all the ingredients together with the dressing. Serve immediately.

Sprout and Bacon Salad

Serves 4

	Metric	Imperial	American
*Streaky bacon rashers
(slices)*	4	4	4
*Brussels sprouts
(more if very small)*	10	10	10
Small onion or shallot	1	1	1

Recommended dressing:

*Oil and vinegar dressing
(see page 117)*	30 ml	2 tbsp	2 tbsp

Grill (broil) the bacon until crisp. Allow to cool and dice. Finely chop the sprouts and onion. Mix all the ingredients together with the dressing and serve.

Sweetcorn and Watercress Salad

Serves 4

	Metric	Imperial	American
Bunch of watercress	*1*	*1*	*1*
Can mixed corn with			
(bell) peppers, drained	*200 g*	*7 oz*	*7 oz*
Recommended dressing:			
Oil and vinegar dressing			
(see page 117)	*30 ml*	*2 tbsp*	*2 tbsp*
Salt and pepper			

Coarsely chop the watercress and mix with the corn with peppers. Toss in the dressing and season to taste.

Raw Mushroom Salad

Serves 4

	Metric	Imperial	American
Button mushrooms	*225 g*	*8 oz*	*8 oz*
Chopped fresh parsley	*60 ml*	*4 tbsp*	*4 tbsp*
Recommended dressing:			
French dressing			
(see page 117)	*45 ml*	*3 tbsp*	*3 tbsp*
Pepper			

Wash and dry the mushrooms. Slice finely and sprinkle with the parsley. Pour over the dressing and leave to marinate for 1 hour, turning from time to time. Sprinkle with pepper before serving.

Raw Beetroot Salad

Serves 4

	Metric	Imperial	American
Large beetroot (red beet), raw	1	1	1
Oil	15 ml	1 tbsp	1 tbsp
Lemon juice	15 ml	1 tbsp	1 tbsp
Salt and pepper			

Peel and grate the raw beetroot. Mix with the oil and lemon juice. Season to taste.

Try other root vegetables such as turnips, swedes or celeriac in the same way.

COOKED SALADS

The recipes in this section are made up mainly of cooked ingredients served cold in a variety of dressings. They are suitable for starters or salad medleys. Increase the dressing quantities if you prefer moister, more strongly-flavoured salads – experiment to taste!

Asparagus and Soya Bean Salad

Serves 4

	Metric	Imperial	American
Soya beans	100 g	4 oz	½ cup
Canned asparagus tips	280 g	10 oz	10 oz
Celery sticks (ribs)	2	2	2
Carrot	1	1	1
Recommended dressing:			
Oil and vinegar dressing (see page 117)	45 ml	3 tbsp	3 tbsp
Salt and pepper			
To garnish:			
Fresh chopped basil			

Soak the soya beans overnight. Drain and cover with fresh water. Bring to the boil. Boil rapidly for 10 minutes, reduce heat and simmer for 2 hours or until cooked. Drain and rinse with cold water. Drain again. Chop the asparagus and celery and mix with the cold beans. Grate the carrot and add to the salad mixture, together with the dressing. Season to taste. Garnish with chopped fresh basil.

Canadian Artichoke Salad

Serves 4

	Metric	Imperial	American
Jerusalem artichokes	225 g	8 oz	8 oz
Bunch of watercress	1	1	1
Grated raw beetroot (red beet)	1	1	1
Recommended dressing:			
Oil and vinegar dressing (see page 117)	30 ml	2 tbsp	2 tbsp
Salt and pepper			

Boil the artichokes in salted water for 8–10 minutes. They should remain firm. Allow to cool and scrape off the skins. Dice and mix with the coarsely chopped watercress and grated beetroot. Toss in the dressing and season to taste before serving.

Celeriac Salad

Serves 4

	Metric	Imperial	American
Celeriac	1	1	1
Spring onions (scallions)	2	2	2
Green (bell) pepper	¼	¼	¼
Chopped fresh parsley	15 ml	1 tbsp	1 tbsp
Recommended dressing:			
Vinaigrette dressing (see page 118)	30 ml	2 tbsp	2 tbsp
Salt and pepper			

Simmer the sliced celeriac in salted water for 10 minutes. Drain and allow to cool. Then cut into sticks or small cubes. Finely chop the spring onions, green pepper and parsley and mix with the celeriac. Toss in vinaigrette and season to taste.

Cooked Vegetable Salad

Serves 4

	Metric	Imperial	American
Frozen peas	*60 ml*	*4 tbsp*	*4 tbsp*
Frozen haricot vert	*45 ml*	*3 tbsp*	*3 tbsp*
Can of asparagus	*280 g*	*7 oz*	*7 oz*
Can of artichoke hearts	*180 g*	*6½ oz*	*6½ oz*
Recommended dressing:			
Oil and lemon dressing			
(see page 117)	*45 ml*	*3 tbsp*	*3 tbsp*
Salt and pepper			
To garnish:			
Hard-boiled			
(hard-cooked) eggs	*2*	*2*	*2*
Chopped fresh parsley			

Cook the peas and beans, drain and allow to cool. Chop the asparagus and artichokes into small pieces and toss in the dressing. Season to taste. Chop the hard-boiled eggs and sprinkle over the top with chopped parsley.

Crab and Rice Salad

Serves 4

	Metric	Imperial	American
Long-grain rice	*60 ml*	*4 tbsp*	*4 tbsp*
Celery sticks (ribs)	*3*	*3*	*3*
Capers	*5 ml*	*1 tsp*	*1 tsp*
Brown and white *crab meat*	*100 g*	*4 oz*	*1 cup*
Recommended dressing:			
Oil and vinegar dressing *(see page 117)*	*30 ml*	*2 tbsp*	*2 tbsp*
Pepper			

Cook the rice in boiling, salted water for 10–15 minutes until tender. Drain, rinse with cold water and drain again. Finely chop the celery and capers and mix with the crab meat and the dressing. Season with pepper to taste. Pile onto rice and serve.

Italian Ham and Potato Salad

Serves 4

	Metric	Imperial	American
New potatoes	*350 g*	*12 oz*	*12 oz*
Cooked ham, diced	*100 g*	*4 oz*	*½ cup*
Cooked peas	*45 ml*	*3 tbsp*	*3 tbsp*
Recommended dressing:			
Honeyed Italian dressing *(see page 122)*	*30 ml*	*2 tbsp*	*2 tbsp*
Pepper			

Cook the potatoes, drain and allow to cool. Dice and mix with the diced ham and peas. Toss all together in the dressing. Sprinkle with black pepper then serve.

Oriental Sesame Chicken Salad

Serves 4

	Metric	Imperial	American
Sesame seeds	15 ml	1 tbsp	1 tbsp
Boneless chicken breasts	3	3	3
Water	1.5 l	2½ pts	6 cups
Soy sauce	15 ml	1 tbsp	1 tbsp
Salt	2.5 ml	½ tsp	½ tsp
Five-spice powder	2.5 ml	½ tsp	½ tsp
Celery sticks (ribs)	3	3	3

Recommended dressing:
*Oriental-style Dressing
  (see page 123)*

Sprinkle the sesame seeds into a small, shallow baking tin (pan) and bake in a preheated oven at 180°/350°F/ gas mark 4 for about 5 minutes or until golden. Place the chicken, water, Soy sauce, salt and five-spice powder in a large saucepan. Bring to the boil, cover and simmer for 20 minutes. Remove from the heat and allow the chicken to stand in the cooking liquid for 1 hour. Remove the chicken, reserving the stock and cut the meat into thick slices. Bring the stock back up to the boil, add the celery and cook for about 2 minutes until crisp but tender. Drain well and add to the chicken. Toss in the Oriental-style dressing and sprinkle with sesame seeds.

Note: Use the stock for a Chinese-style soup.

Dutch Beet and Potato Salad

Serves 4

	Metric	Imperial	American
Cooked beetroot (red beet)	2	2	2
Cooked potatoes	2	2	2
Hard-boiled (hard-cooked) eggs	2	2	2
Crisp green apple	1	1	1
Gherkins	2	2	2
Recommended dressing:			
Mayonnaise (see page 119)	45 ml	3 tbsp	3 tbsp
Dash of vinegar			
Salt and pepper			

Dice all the ingredients and mix together with the mayonnaise and vinegar. The consistency should be fairly solid. Add salt and pepper to taste. This recipe makes a good side salad to cold meats.

German Potato Salad

Serves 4

	Metric	Imperial	American
Potatoes	450 g	1 lb	1 lb
Gherkins, finely chopped	2	2	2
Recommended dressing:			
Oil and vinegar dressing (see page 117)	45 ml	3 tbsp	3 tbsp
Salt and pepper			

Boil the potatoes in their skins until tender, then peel and chop coarsely. Mix in the finely chopped gherkin and dressing while the potatoes are still hot. Add seasoning to taste and leave to cool before serving.

French Potato Salad

Serves 4

	Metric	*Imperial*	*American*
Potatoes	*450 g*	*1 lb*	*1 lb*
Small onion,			
finely chopped	*1*	*1*	*1*
Chopped fresh parsley			
Recommended dressing:			
Oil and vinegar dressing			
(see page 117)	*45 ml*	*3 tbsp*	*3 tbsp*
Salt and pepper			
To garnish:			
Chopped (snipped) chives			

Boil the potatoes in their skins until tender, then peel and chop coarsely. Mix in the finely chopped onion and parsley and dressing while the potatoes are still hot. Add seasoning to taste and leave to cool before serving, garnished with chopped chives.

Russian Salad

Serves 4

	Metric	Imperial	American
Cooked peas	45 ml	3 tbsp	3 tbsp
Cooked potatoes	2	2	2
Cooked carrots	2	2	2
Cooked runner beans	45 ml	3 tbsp	3 tbsp
Cooked turnip	1	1	1

Recommended dressing:

Mayonnaise (see page 119)	45 ml	3 tbsp	3 tbsp

Salt and pepper

To garnish:

Anchovy fillets
Capers
Chopped fresh parsley

Put the peas in a bowl. Dice all the remaining vegetables and add to the peas. Mix with the mayonnaise and season to taste. Pile onto a serving dish. Garnish with anchovy fillets, capers and chopped parsley and chill before serving.

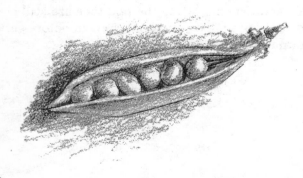

Haricot Bean Salad

Serves 4

	Metric	*Imperial*	*American*
Haricot beans	*75 g*	*3 oz*	*½ cup*
Onion	*½*	*½*	*½*
Celery stick (rib)	*½*	*½*	*½*
Gherkin	*1*	*1*	*1*
Tomatoes	*2*	*2*	*2*
Worcestershire sauce (optional)	*5 ml*	*1 tsp*	*1 tsp*

Recommended dressing:
Garlic dressing
  (see page 121)
To garnish:
Chopped fresh parsley

Soak the beans in cold water overnight. Drain and place in a pan with fresh water. Bring to the boil, boil rapidly for 10 minutes then simmer for 1½ hours, drain and cool. Finely chop the onion, celery, gherkin and tomatoes and mix with the beans. Toss in Worcestershire sauce if using, then Garlic dressing. Sprinkle with chopped parsley to garnish before serving.

Haricot Bean and Parsley Salad

Serves 4

	Metric	Imperial	American
Haricot beans	*100 g*	*4 oz*	*⅔ cup*
Recommended dressing:			
French dressing			
(see page 117)	*30 ml*	*2 tbsp*	*2 tbsp*
Salt and pepper			
Chopped fresh parsley	*45 ml*	*3 tbsp*	*3 tbsp*

Soak the beans in cold water overnight. Drain and place in a pan with fresh water. Bring to the boil and boil rapidly for 10 minutes then simmer for 1½ hours, drain and leave to cool. Toss in the dressing. Season and sprinkle with the parsley. Try also with butter beans, black eyed beans or soya beans.

Haricot Verts Vinaigrette

Serves 4

	Metric	Imperial	American
Fresh or frozen			
haricot verts	*450 g*	*1 lb*	*1 lb*
Small onion	*1*	*1*	*1*
Recommended dressing:			
Vinaigrette dressing			
(see page 118)	*75 ml*	*6 tbsp*	*6 tbsp*
Pepper			

Cook and drain the beans, rinse with cold water and drain again. Finely slice the onion and toss both beans and onion then the dressing. Season with pepper, chill and serve.

Italian Salmon and Pasta Salad

Serves 4

	Metric	*Imperial*	*American*
Pasta shells	*100 g*	*4 oz*	*1 cup*
Can red salmon	*400 g*	*15 oz*	*15 oz*
Canned pimientos	*2*	*2*	*2*
Celery sticks (ribs)	*3*	*3*	*3*
Recommended dressing:			
Oil and vinegar dressing			
(see page 117)	*45 ml*	*3 tbsp*	*3 tbsp*
To garnish:			
Lettuce			
Chopped fresh parsley			

Boil the pasta in plenty of salted water until just tender, drain, rinse with cold water and drain again. Flake the fish, discarding skin and bone. Mix with the pasta shells and chopped pimientos and celery. Toss in the dressing, season then serve on a bed of lettuce and garnish with the chopped parsley.

Use larger quantities of fish and pasta to make an excellent main course for a light meal.

Mushroom and Fennel Salad

Serves 4

	Metric	Imperial	American
Fennel bulb (or celery heart)	1	1	1
Mushrooms, finely sliced	100 g	4 oz	1 cup
Recommended dressing:			
Mayonnaise (see page 119)	30 ml	2 tbsp	2 tbsp
Vinegar	5 ml	1 tsp	1 tsp
Salt and pepper			

Cook the fennel for 5 minutes in boiling, salted water. Drain and leave to cool. Chop and mix with the finely sliced mushrooms. Mix the mayonnaise and vinegar, add to the vegetables and toss. Serve on a bed of lettuce.

Jerusalem Artichoke Salad

Serves 4

	Metric	Imperial	American
Jerusalem artichokes	4	4	4
Leeks	2	2	2
Potatoes	2	2	2
Recommended dressing:			
Yoghurt dressing (see page 121)	60 ml	4 tbsp	4 tbsp
Streaky bacon rashers (slices)	2	2	2

Boil the artichokes and leeks for 7 and 4 minutes respectively in salted water. Boil the potatoes, then allow all vegetables to cool. Dice and mix together with the dressing and leave to stand for 1 hour before serving. Sprinkle with the chopped crisply fried bacon.

Savoury Rice

Serves 4

	Metric	Imperial	American
Long-grain rice	*75 g*	*3 oz*	*⅓ cup*
Green (bell) pepper	*½*	*½*	*½*
Mushrooms, chopped	*100 g*	*4 oz*	*1 cup*
Sweetcorn (corn), canned or frozen	*225 g*	*8 oz*	*2 cups*
Recommended dressing:			
Oil and vinegar dressing (see page 117)	*30 ml*	*2 tbsp*	*2 tbsp*
Salt and pepper			

Cook the rice in plenty of boiling, salted water. Drain, rinse with cold water and drain again. Finely chop the green pepper and mushrooms and add to the rice with the sweetcorn. Toss in the dressing and season to taste.

Prawn (Shrimp) and Potato Salad

Serves 4

	Metric	*Imperial*	*American*
Potatoes	*450 g*	*1 lb*	*1 lb*
Can of prawns (shrimp)			
in brine	*200 g*	*7 oz*	*7 oz*
Recommended dressing:			
Sour cream dressing			
(see page 121)	*30 ml*	*2 tbsp*	*2 tbsp*
Salt and pepper			
To garnish:			
Chopped (snipped) chives			

Boil and peel the potatoes then mix with the drained prawns and soured cream dressing. Season to taste. For a slightly different flavour mix 5 ml/1 tsp tomato purée (paste) with the dressing before mixing with the other ingredients. Garnish with chopped chives before serving.

Turn this recipe into a delicious light lunch by adding a small can of drained sweetcorn (corn) with (bell) peppers and serving with a green salad (see page 102).

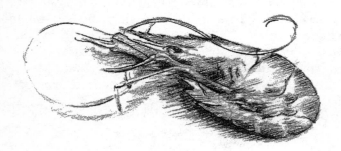

SAVOURY SALADS WITH FRUIT

Fruit in savoury salads is refreshing and can add a additional dimension. The recipes in this selection can be used on their own, as starters or in salad medleys. One or two also make good main course dishes.

Apple, Cream Cheese and Date Salad

Serves 4

	Metric	Imperial	American
Eating (dessert) apples	4	4	4
Juice of lemon	½	½	½
Dates	50 g	2 oz	⅓ cup
Walnuts	50 g	2 oz	⅓ cup
Cream cheese	100 g	4 oz	½ cup
Recommended dressing:			
Mayonnaise			
(see page 119)	30 ml	2 tbsp	2 tbsp

Core and chop the apples and sprinkle with lemon juice to stop the fruit discolouring. Chop the dates and walnuts and add to the apples. Mix the cream cheese with the mayonnaise and then mix in the fruit. Chill, if time before serving.

Avocado and Tomato Salad

Serves 4

	Metric	Imperial	American
Large ripe avocado	1	1	1
Recommended dressing:			
Vinaigrette dressing (see page 118)	30 ml	2 tbsp	2 tbsp
Tomatoes	3	3	3
Cucumber	10 cm	4 in	4 in
To garnish:			
Watercress			

Peel, stone (pit), and chop the avocado and add the dressing as quickly as possible to prevent discolouration. Chop the tomatoes and cucumber and add to the avocado. Toss together well and serve chilled garnished with watercress. For extra flavour add 10 ml/ 2 tsp Worcestershire sauce to the Vinaigrette.

Crunchy Pear Salad

Serves 4

	Metric	Imperial	American
Small Iceberg lettuce	½	½	½
Ripe eating (dessert) pears	2	2	2
Lemon juice	15 ml	1 tbsp	1 tbsp
Celery sticks (ribs)	2	2	2
Walnuts, chopped	50 g	2 oz	½ cup
Raisins	50 g	2 oz	⅓ cup
Cottage cheese	225 g	8 oz	1 cup
Recommended dressing:			
Mayonnaise (see page 119)	150 ml	¼ pt	⅔ cup

Shred the lettuce and arrange on a serving plate. Halve and core the pears and brush with the lemon juice to prevent discolouring. Arrange them with the lettuce on the plate. Mix the remaining ingredients well and pile them onto the pears.

Avocado and Crab Salad

Serves 4

	Metric	Imperial	American
Avocados	2	2	2
Fresh dressed crab	1	1	1
Green (bell) pepper	½	½	½
Recommended dressing:			
Mayonnaise (see page 119)	30 ml	2 tbsp	2 tbsp
Salt and pepper			
To garnish:			
Lettuce			

Peel and stone (pit) the avocados. Chop and mix with crab meat and mayonnaise as quickly as possible to avoid discolouration. Finely chop the green pepper and add to the avocado and crab mixture. Season to taste. Pile onto a bed of lettuce in individual dishes. Makes a good starter or light lunch.

Californian Fruit Salad

Serves 4

	Metric	Imperial	American
Can of pineapple chunks	215 g	7½ oz	7½ oz
Can of peaches	215 g	7½ oz	7½ oz
Celery sticks (ribs)	4	4	4
Flaked almonds	45 ml	3 tbsp	3 tbsp

Recommended dressing:
Cheese mayonnaise
(see page 120)
To garnish:
Lettuce

Chop all the ingredients and mix with mayonnaise. Serve on a bed of lettuce. Fresh fruit can be used if preferred.

Cheese Stuffed Peaches

Serves 4

	Metric	Imperial	American
Can of peaches	410 g	14½ oz	14½ oz
or fresh peaches	4	4	4
Filling:			
Cream cheese	100 g	4 oz	1 cup
A little milk (optional)			
Celery stick (rib)	1	1	1
Dates, stoned			
(pitted)	50 g	2 oz	⅓ cup
Salt and pepper			

Moisten the cream cheese with a little juice from the peaches or a little milk. Chop the celery and dates finely and mix with the cheese. Season and pile into the peach halves.

Trying adding chopped walnuts to the cheese mixture, or pear halves instead of peaches. Use the cheese mixture on its own too.

Chicory and Peach Salad

Serves 4

	Metric	*Imperial*	*American*
Chicory (endive) heads	*3*	*3*	*3*
Flaked almonds	*15 ml*	*1 tbsp*	*1 tbsp*
Raisins	*15 ml*	*1 tbsp*	*1 tbsp*
Small can of peaches	*215 g*	*7½ oz*	*7½ oz*
Recommended dressing:			
Garlic dressing (see page 121)	*30 ml*	*2 tbsp*	*2 tbsp*
Salt and pepper			

Chop the chicory and mix with the nuts and raisins. Dice the peaches and add to the salad. Toss all the ingredients in the dressing and season to taste.

Chicken with Melon

Serves 4

	Metric	Imperial	American
Diced cooked chicken	225 g	8 oz	1 cup
Cantaloupe or Ogen melon	½	½	½
White grapes	100 g	4 oz	⅔ cup
Recommended dressing:			

Soured (dairy sour)
  cream dressing
  (see page 121)
	30 ml	2 tbsp	2 tbsp

Salt and pepper			
To garnish:			
Lettuce			

Cut the grapes in half and remove pips (pits). Dice the melon and mix with the chicken and grapes. Add soured cream dressing and season to taste. Serve on a bed of lettuce.

A larger quantity makes a good main course.

Grape and Mushroom Salad

Serves 4

	Metric	Imperial	American
White grapes	350 g	12 oz	1⅓ cups
Button mushrooms	175 g	6 oz	6 oz
Carton of natural (plain) yoghurt	150 ml	¼ pt	⅔ cup
Salt and pepper			
Chopped fresh mint	10 ml	2 tsp	2 tsp

Cut the grapes in half and remove the pips (pits). Finely slice the mushrooms and mix with grapes and yoghurt. Season to taste and add the mint. Serve well chilled in individual dishes or glasses. Try adding a crushed clove of garlic to the yoghurt for a more continental flavour.

Chicory and Orange Salad

Serves 4

	Metric	Imperial	American
Small oranges	4	4	4
Chicory (endive) heads	4	4	4
Black olives, halved and stoned (pitted)	20	20	20
Recommended dressing:			
Honeyed Italian dressing (see page 122)	30 ml	2 tbsp	2 tbsp

Peel the oranges and remove all traces of the pith. Cut into rounds and then into four. Coarsely chop the chicory and mix with the oranges and olives. Toss in the dressing. This is also good with about six Chinese leaves in place of the chicory.

Grape, Melon and Mint Salad

Serves 4

	Metric	Imperial	American
White grapes	100 g	4 oz	⅔ cup
Honeydew melon	½	½	½
Chopped fresh mint	10 ml	2 tsp	2 tsp
Recommended dressing:			
Oil and vinegar dressing (see page 117)	60 ml	4 tbsp	4 tbsp

Cut the grapes in half and remove the pips (pits). Scoop the seeds from the melon then peel and chop into cubes. Mix the grapes and melon and sprinkle with the mint and dressing. Chill before serving.

Grape and Celery Salad

Serves 4

	Metric	Imperial	American
White grapes	225 g	8 oz	1⅓ cups
Cucumber	7.5 cm	3 in	3 in
Celery sticks (ribs)	2	2	2
Green (bell) pepper	½	½	½
Natural (plain) yoghurt	45 ml	3 tbsp	3 tbsp
Chopped fresh rosemary			
Salt and pepper			

Cut the grapes in half and remove the pips (pits). Finely dice the cucumber, celery and green pepper. Mix all the ingredients together with the rosemary and yoghurt. Season to taste with salt and pepper.

Grape and Fennel Salad with Prawns (Shrimp)

Serves 4

	Metric	Imperial	American
Fennel bulb	1	1	1
White grapes	225 g	8 oz	1⅓ cups
Recommended dressing:			
Soured (dairy sour)			
cream dressing			
(see page 121)	30 ml	2 tbsp	2 tbsp
Salt and pepper			

Slice then parboil the fennel for 5 minutes. Drain and cool. Halve the grapes and remove the pips (pits). Mix with the chopped fennel. Add the soured cream dressing and season to taste.

Grapefruit and Avocado Salad

Serves 4

	Metric	Imperial	American
Grapefruit	1	1	1
Ripe avocados	2	2	2
Recommended dressing:			
French dressing			
(see page 117)	30 ml	2 tbsp	2 tbsp
To garnish:			
Chopped fresh parsley			

Peel the grapefruit, making sure all the pith is removed, and chop coarsely. Peel and slice the avocados and mix with the grapefruit. Work quickly so that the avocado does not discolour. Marinate in the dressing and serve well-chilled, garnished with parsley.

Melon Salad

Serves 4

	Metric	Imperial	American
Honeydew melon, seeded and peeled	¼	¼	¼
Eating (dessert) apples, (cored)	2	2	2
Celery sticks (ribs)	2	2	2
Chopped walnuts	25 g	1 oz	¼ cup
Recommended dressing:			
Soured (dairy sour) cream dressing (see page 121)	30 ml	2 tbsp	2 tbsp
Salt and pepper			

Cut the melon and apple into small chunks and mix with the finely chopped celery and walnuts. Add the soured cream dressing and season to taste.

Mandarin Ham Salad

Serves 4

	Metric	Imperial	American
Uncooked long-grain rice	90 ml	6 tbsp	6 tbsp
Tomato	1	1	1
Cooked ham	100 g	4 oz	4 oz
Can of mandarin oranges	300 g	11 oz	11 oz
Recommended dressing:			
Vinaigrette dressing (see page 118)	30 ml	2 tbsp	2 tbsp
Pepper			

Cook the rice, drain, rinse with cold water and drain again. Chop the tomato and dice the ham. Drain the oranges. Mix with all the other ingredients and toss in the vinaigrette and plenty of pepper.

Melon and Tomato Salad

Serves 4

	Metric	Imperial	American
Tomatoes	4	4	4
Cucumber	¼	¼	¼
Honeydew melon, seeded and peeled	½	½	½
Recommended dressing:			
Oil and vinegar dressing (see page 117)	30 ml	2 tbsp	2 tbsp
Fresh, chopped basil	10 ml	2 tsp	2 tsp
Salt and pepper			

Skin and roughly chop the tomatoes. Cube the cucumber and melon and mix with the tomatoes. Toss in the dressing with the basil and season to taste.

Melon and Salmon Salad

Serves 4

	Metric	Imperial	American
Cooked fresh salmon	225 g	8 oz	8 oz
White grapes	100 g	4 oz	⅔ cup
Charentais melon	½	½	½

Recommended dressing:

Mayonnaise flavoured with paprika (see page 119)	30 ml	2 tbsp	2 tbsp

To garnish:

Lettuce
Whole prawns (shrimp)
Chopped fresh parsley

Flake the fish and remove any bones and skin. Halve the grapes and remove the pips (pits). Dice the melon. Mix all the ingredients with the dressing and pile on to a bed of lettuce on individual dishes. Decorate with whole prawns and chopped parsley.

Thai Salad

Serves 4

	Metric	Imperial	American
Can of pineapple chunks	225 g	8 oz	8 oz
Celery sticks (ribs)	4	4	4
Cooking (tart) apple, peeled	1	1	1
Small green or red (bell) pepper	1	1	1

Recommended dressing:

Oil and vinegar dressing (see page 117)	30 ml	2 tbsp	2 tbsp

Salt and pepper

To garnish: *Roasted peanuts*

Chop all the ingredients finely and mix together. Toss in the dressing and season to taste. Sprinkle with roasted peanuts just before serving. This recipe makes a good starter or can be used in a salad medley. Try adding diced cooked chicken to make it into a light main course.

Mushroom and Apple Salad

Serves 4

	Metric	Imperial	American
Eating (dessert) apple	1	1	1
Juice of lemon	1	1	1
Mushrooms	100 g	4 oz	4 oz
Can of sweet corn (corn)	325 g	11 oz	11 oz
Cucumber	10 cm	4 in	4 in
Raisins	25 g	1 oz	1 oz
Recommended dressing:			
Garlic dressing (see page 121)	30 ml	2 tbsp	2 tbsp
Salt and pepper			

Chop the apples and mix with a little lemon juice to stop them discolouring. Chop the mushrooms and cucumber and mix together with the apples, sweetcorn and raisins. Toss in garlic dressing and season to taste.

Polynesian Chicken Salad

Serves 4

	Metric	Imperial	American
Garlic clove	1	1	1
Cooked long-grain rice	100 g	4 oz	good cup
Cooked chicken, diced	450 g	1 lb	2 cups
Canned pineapple chunks	225 g	8 oz	8 o
Spring onions (scallions)	4	4	4
Green (bell) pepper	1	1	1
Olive oil	30 ml	2 tbsp	2 tbsp
Pineapple juice	15 ml	1 tbsp	1 tbsp

To garnish: Watercress

Rub the salad bowl with the split clove of garlic. Mix the rice with all the other finely diced ingredients and the dressing. Garnish with watercress.

Clementine and Cream Cheese

Serves 4

	Metric	Imperial	American
Clementines	4	4	4
Cream cheese	100 g	4 oz	½ cup
A little milk			
Flaked almonds	15 ml	1 tbsp	1 tbsp
Raisins	15 ml	1 tbsp	1 tbsp
Salt and pepper			

To garnish: Watercress

Peel the clementines and open into sections without separating totally. Remove the pith and cores. Mix the cream cheese with a little milk, the almonds and raisins then season to taste. Pile in the centre of each clementine. Garnish with watercress. This recipe makes an unusual starter.

Melon and Watercress Salad

Serves 4

	Metric	Imperial	American
Streakey bacon rashers (slices)	4	4	4
Bunch watercress	1	1	1
Honeydew melon	½	½	½
Recommended dressing:			
Oil and vinegar dressing (see page 117)	30 ml	2 tbsp	2 tbsp
Pepper			

Grill (broil) the bacon until crispy. Allow to cool then dice. Coarsely chop the watercress and peel, de-seed and dice the melon. Add the bacon and toss in the dressing. Grind plenty of pepper over before serving.

Mexican Banana Salad

Serves 4

	Metric	Imperial	American
Bananas	*4*	*4*	*4*
Juice of lemon	*1*	*1*	*1*
Oranges	*2*	*2*	*2*
Dates, stoned (pitted)	*75 g*	*3 oz*	*½ cup*
Walnut halves	*50 g*	*2 oz*	*½ cup*
Pickled chilli (chili)	*1*	*1*	*1*
Recommended dressing:			
Mayonnaise (see page 119)	*30 ml*	*2 tbsp*	*2 tbsp*
To garnish:			
Cos (romaine) lettuce			
Cayenne pepper			

Cut bananas into chunks and toss in lemon juice to
prevent discolouration. Remove all peel and pith from
oranges and cut into segments. Add to bananas with
any juice. Add halved dates, roughly chopped walnuts
and finely chopped chilli. Mix with mayonnaise. Tear
lettuce into pieces and place on serving plates. Pile
salad on top and sprinkle with cayenne pepper.

SIDE SALADS

These recipes are designed to be served with the main course of a meal, usually on a separate dish. Ring the changes on a basic green side salad by using a variety of salad leaves and vegetables.

Side salads can be served on individual plates or in a large bowl.

Chestnut and Celery Salad

Serves 4

	Metric	Imperial	American
Chestnuts	20	20	20
Celery sticks (ribs)	4	4	4
Chopped fresh parsley			
Recommended dressing:			
Honeyed Italian dressing			
(see page 122)	30 ml	2 tbsp	2 tbsp

Place the chestnuts in a pan of water and boil until cooked. Strip off skin with a knife and leave to cool. Finely chop all the ingredients and combine with the dressing. This salad goes particularly well with cold turkey. Drained canned chestnuts can be used instead of fresh.

Cucumber and Yoghurt Salad

	Metric	Imperial	American
Per person:			
Mint leaves	6	6	6
Natural (plain) yoghurt	15 ml	1 tbsp	1 tbsp
Salt and pepper			
Cucumber	5 cm	2 in	2 in

Finely chop the mint and mix with the yoghurt and seasoning. Slice or dice the cucumber and place in a dish. Pour over the yoghurt mixture and serve cold.

Cooked Salad Platter

An assortment of cooked:
Artichoke hearts
Carrots
Beetroot (red beet)
Swede or turnip
Asparagus
Haricot verts
Peas
Broad (Lima) beans
Recommended dressing:
Oil and vinegar dressing (see page 117)

Chop the carrots and beetroot. Toss each vegetable separately in the oil and vinegar dressing. Arrange in piles on a large plate. This platter is useful for using up any leftover cooked vegetables. Try adding cauliflower and mushrooms for a change. Also ring the changes with your favourite dressing.

Beetroot in Yoghurt

Serves 4

	Metric	Imperial	American
Spring onions (scallions)			
or shallots	2	2	2
Natural (plain) yoghurt	30 ml	2 tbsp	2 tbsp
Salt and pepper			
Large cooked beetroot			
(red beet)	2	2	2

Finely chop the onions and mix with the yoghurt and seasoning. Dice or slice the cooked beetroot and pour over the yoghurt and onion dressing.

Chicory with Rosemary

Serves 4

	Metric	Imperial	American
Chicory (endive) head			
per person	1	1	1
Pinch of dried rosemary			
Recommended dressing:			
Oil and vinegar dressing			
(see page 117)	45 ml	3 tbsp	3 tbsp

Coarsely chop the chicory and place in individual dishes. Sprinkle with the rosemary and mix with the oil and vinegar dressing.

Cucumber and Olive Salad

Serves 4

	Metric	Imperial	American
Small cucumber	1	1	1
Salt and pepper			
Chopped (snipped) chives	60 ml	4 tbsp	4 tbsp
Soured (dairy sour) cream	250 ml	8 fl oz	1 cup
Sugar	5 ml	1 tsp	1 tsp
Vinegar	15 ml	1 tbsp	1 tbsp
Black olives	8	8	8

To garnish: *a few extra olives and chives*

Finely slice or dice the cucumber. Sprinkle with salt and leave for 1 hour, then rinse and dry. Mix together all the other ingredients and stir in the cucumber. Garnish with a few extra olives and chopped chives.

French Tomato Salad

Serves 4

	Metric	Imperial	American
Beef tomatoes	450 g	1 lb	1 lb
Onion, finely chopped or sliced	½	½	½
Green (bell) pepper	¼	¼	¼
Recommended dressing:			
French dressing (see page 117)	30 ml	2 tbsp	2 tbsp

To garnish: *Parsley*

Peel and slice the tomatoes. Place in a dish and sprinkle with the onions and green pepper. Pour over the dressing and garnish with chopped parsley.

Orange and Onion Salad

Serves 4

	Metric	Imperial	American
Fresh oranges	3	3	3
or can of mandarins	300 g	11 oz	11 oz
Spanish onion	1	1	1

Recommended dressing:

	Metric	Imperial	American
French dressing			
(see page 117)	30 ml	2 tbsp	2 tbsp

Pinch of ground coriander (cilantro)
Paprika
To garnish: *Black olives*

Peel the oranges and remove all the pith. Chop into bite-sized pieces. Finely slice the onion. Mix together and pour over the dressing and add the coriander and paprika. Garnish with a few olives.

Green Cabbage Coleslaw

Serves 4

	Metric	Imperial	American
Small green cabbage	½	½	½
Carrot, grated	1	1	1
Almond flakes	50 g	2 oz	½ cup

Recommended dressing:

	Metric	Imperial	American
Green onion dressing			
(see page 123)	30 ml	2 tbsp	2 tbsp

Salt and pepper

Slice the cabbage as finely as possible and mix with the grated carrot. Add the almond flakes and dressing and season to taste.

General Salad Platter

Serves 4

	Metric	Imperial	American
Lettuce	½	½	½
Bunch of watercress			
or box of cress	½	½	½
Tomatoes	4	4	4
Hard-boiled			
(hard-cooked) eggs	2	2	2
Cucumber	5 cm	2 in	2 in
Radishes	8	8	8
Chopped fresh parsley			
Recommended dressing:			
Oil and vinegar dressing			
(see page 117)	30 ml	2 tbsp	2 tbsp

Tear the lettuce into pieces and cover the base of a large platter. Dot with piles of watercress or cress. Slice the tomatoes, eggs, cucumber and radishes and arrange on top. Sprinkle with parsley or other fresh herbs and pour over your favourite dressing.

Green Side Salad

Serves 4

	Metric	Imperial	American
Bunch of watercress	1	1	1
Chicory (endive) heads	2	2	2
Green (bell) pepper	½	½	½
Cucumber	10 cm	4 in	4 in
Dressing of your choice			

Coarsely chop the watercress and chicory and arrange in four bowls. Add slivers of green pepper and diced cucumber. Just before serving pour over the dressing of your choice. If you are using a plain dressing, use fresh parsley or mint for extra flavour. You might like to add a dash of colour by grating some raw carrot on top before adding the dressing.

Mixed Vegetable Coleslaw

Serves 4

	Metric	Imperial	American
Small white cabbage	½	½	½
Flaked almonds	45 ml	3 tbsp	3 tbsp
Raisins (optional)	30 ml	2 tbsp	2 tbsp
Small, finely sliced green (bell) pepper	¼	¼	¼
Carrot, grated	1	1	1
Shallot or small onion, thinly sliced	1	1	1
Recommended dressing:			
Mayonnaise (see page 119)	45 ml	3 tbsp	3 tbsp
Wine vinegar or lemon juice	10 ml	2 tsp	2 tsp

Shred the cabbage as finely as possible. Add the nuts, raisins, green pepper, carrot and onion and mix with the mayonnaise and vinegar. Season to taste. Add a little mustard to the mayonnaise if desired.

Try combinations of other grated root vegetables, dried fruit and nuts to your own taste or according to availability.

Raw Salad Platter

An assortment of:
Beetroot
Carrot
Radishes
Turnip
Celeriac
Recommended dressing:
Oil and vinegar dressing (see page 117)
To garnish: *Fresh chopped parsley*

Grate each vegetable and mix with oil and vinegar.
Place in individual piles on a large platter. Garnish
with parsley. Experiment with other root vegetables
like swede, salsify, parsnip and so on.

Creamy Red Cabbage Salad

Serves 4

	Metric	Imperial	American
Small red cabbage, grated	¼	¼	¼
Large celery stick (rib)	1	1	1
Finely chopped shallot	1	1	1
or spring onions (scallions)	3	3	3
Chopped walnuts	25 g	1 oz	¼ cup
Soured (dairy sour)			
cream	30 ml	2 tbsp	2 tbsp
Salt and pepper			

Mix the grated cabbage, chopped celery, shallot and
walnuts. Toss in the soured cream and season.

Plain Coleslaw

Serves 4

	Metric	Imperial	American
Small white cabbage	½	½	½
Flaked almonds	45 ml	3 tbsp	3 tbsp
Raisins (optional)	30 ml	2 tbsp	2 tbsp
Recommended dressing:			
Mayonnaise			
(see page 119)	45 ml	3 tbsp	3 tbsp
Wine vinegar or			
lemon juice	10 ml	2 tsp	2 tsp
Salt and pepper			

Shred the cabbage as finely as possible. Revive limp cabbage by standing in cold water after slicing. Add the nuts and raisins and mix together with the mayonnaise and vinegar. Season to taste. Particularly good as a side salad with grills.

Chinese Spinach Salad

Serves 4

	Metric	Imperial	American
Spinach	450 g	1 lb	1 lb
Soy sauce	30 ml	2 tbsp	2 tbsp
Wine vinegar	15 ml	1 tbsp	1 tbsp
Sugar	10 ml	2 tsp	2 tsp
Sesame oil	10 ml	2 tsp	2 tsp
Peanut butter	5 ml	1 tsp	1 tsp

Blanch the spinach in a bowl of boiling water for 2 minutes then drain, rinse in cold water and cut into strips. Mix together all the remaining ingredients and pour over the spinach. Toss together well and chill for 20 minutes before serving.

Watercress and Pimiento Salad

Serves 4

	Metric	Imperial	American
Bunch of watercress	1	1	1
Canned pimientos	2	2	2
Cucumber	5 cm	2 in	2 in
Radishes	8	8	8
Recommended dressing:			
Oil and vinegar dressing (see page 117)	30 ml	2 tbsp	2 tbsp

Chop all the ingredients and toss together in the dressing.

Sunshine Salad

Serves 4

	Metric	Imperial	American
Hard-boiled (hard-cooked) eggs	2	2	2
Mushrooms	50 g	2 oz	2 oz
Can sweetcorn (corn)	200 g	7 oz	7 oz
Salt and pepper			
Carrots	100 g	4 oz	4 oz
French mustard	2.5 ml	½ tsp	½ tsp
Soured (dairy sour) cream	30 ml	2 tbsp	2 tbsp
Oil or lemon juice			

To garnish:
Chopped fresh parsley

Separate the yolks from the white of the eggs. Chop the whites with the mushrooms and mix with the sweetcorn. Season and tip into the centre of a large plate. Grate the carrots and mix with a little oil or lemon juice. Arrange them around the sweetcorn mixture. Mix the mustard, egg yolks and soured cream and pour over the corn mixture. Garnish with chopped parsley.

DESSERT SALADS

There is no more refreshing way to end a meal than with a fruit salad. But if you think that just means a mixture of fruits in a syrup you're about to discover how wrong you can be!

Brandied Dried Fruit Salad

Serves 4

	Metric	Imperial	American
Packed dried fruit salad	*225 g*	*8 oz*	*8 oz*
Cold water	*300 ml*	*½ pt*	*1¼ cups*
Granulated sugar			
(optional)	*50 g*	*2 oz*	*¼ cup*
Brandy	*30 ml*	*2 tbsp*	*2 tbsp*
To serve:			
Crème fraiche			

Put the fruit into a bowl, add the water and leave to soak for at least 4 hours (or overnight). Transfer to a saucepan, add sugar, if using. Bring to the boil, reduce heat, cover and simmer gently for 30 minutes or until tender but not pulpy. Add a little more cold water during cooking if liked. Stir in the brandy and leave to cool. Chill until ready to serve with crème fraiche.

Mixed Fruit Salad Platter

Serves 4

	Metric	*Imperial*	*American*
Ripe Mango	*1*	*1*	*1*
Starfruit	*1*	*1*	*1*
Strawberries	*6*	*6*	*6*
Kiwifruit	*1*	*1*	*1*
Sauce:			
Can raspberries	*300 g*	*11 oz*	*11 oz*
Icing (confectioners')			
sugar	*15 ml*	*1 tbsp*	*1 tbsp*

Peel the mango and cut the fruit off the stone in segments. Slice the starfruit. Hull and halve the strawberries. Sieve the fruit and mix icing sugar into the pulp. Spoon the sauce in a pool on individual serving plates. Arrange fruit attractively on top and serve.

Note: Ring the changes with any selection of fresh fruit you choose.

Oriental Fruit Salad

Serves 4-6

	Metric	Imperial	American
Can lychees	420 g	15 oz	15 oz
Can mandarin oranges	300 ml	11 oz	11 oz
Kiwifruit	2	2	2
Small honeydew melon	½	½	½
Piece stem ginger in syrup	1	1	1
Ginger syrup from jar	15 ml	1 tbsp	1 tbsp

To serve:
Whipped cream

Empty the lychees and mandarins with their syrup into a large bowl. Peel and slice the kiwifruit and add to the bowl. Scoop seeds out of the melon then, using a melon baller, scoop flesh into the bowl. Alternatively, peel, then dice the flesh. Chop the stem ginger and add with the ginger syrup. Mix well then chill. Serve with whipped cream.

Note: For fun, and if you can find them, serve with a plate of fortune cookies.

Pear Tropicana

Serves 4

	Metric	Imperial	American
Ripe eating (dessert) pears	4	4	4

Recommended dressing:
Pineapple and Orange
  dressing (see page 124)
To decorate:
Toasted flaked almonds

Peel and core the pears and cut into slices. Mix with the dressing and spoon into glass serving dishes. Chill. Sprinkle with toasted flaked almonds just before serving.

Storecupboard Supreme Salad

Serves 4

	Metric	Imperial	American
Can mandarin oranges	300 g	11 oz	11 oz
Small can red cherries	220 g	8 oz	8 oz
Can pear quarters	410 g	14½ oz	14½ oz
Lemon juice	15 ml	1 tbsp	1 tbsp
Medium sherry	30 ml	2 tbsp	2 tbsp

Put the mandarins and their juice in a serving dish. Remove stones (pits) from cherries, if necessary, and add to the bowl with their juice. Dice the pears and add with their juice to bowl. Stir in the lemon juice and sherry and chill until ready to serve.

Golden Dream Salad

Serves 4

	Metric	Imperial	American
Oranges	4	4	4
Nectarines	4	4	4
Yellow plums	4	4	4

Recommended dressing:
Sugar-free Dressing
  (see page 124)
To serve:
Apricot fromage frais
Toasted chopped nuts

Peel the oranges, removing all pith. Slice, then cut the slices into quarters. Halve the nectarines, remove stones (pits) and slice. Repeat with the plums. Mix lightly in a bowl. Pour dressing over and chill for at least 2 hours to let flavours develop. Spoon into individual serving dishes. Serve each portion with a spoonful of apricot fromage frais on top and a few chopped toasted nuts.

Green Fruit Salad

Serves 4

	Metric	Imperial	American
Cantaloupe melon	*1*	*1*	*1*
White grapes	*225 g*	*8 oz*	*1⅓ cups*
Green eating (dessert)			
* apples*	*2*	*2*	*2*
Lemon juice	*30 ml*	*2 tbsp*	*2 tbsp*
Kiwifruit	*2*	*2*	*2*

Recommended dressing:
White Wine Syrup dressing
* (see page 125)*

To serve:
Whipped cream

Peel, remove seeds and cube the melon (or use a melon baller). Place in a large serving bowl. Cut the grapes in halves, remove pips (pits) and add to the melon. Halve and core the apple, but do not peel. Cut in small dice and toss in the lemon juice. Add to the bowl. Peel, halve and slice the kiwifruit. Pour cold wine dressing over and chill for at least 1 hour. Serve with whipped cream.

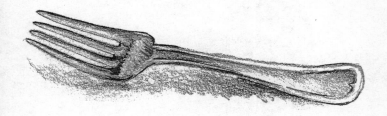

Strawberry Syllabub Salad

Serves 4

	Metric	*Imperial*	*American*
Strawberries	*350 g*	*12 oz*	*12 oz*
Orange liqueur	*30 ml*	*2 tbsp*	*2 tbsp*
Caster (superfine) sugar (optional)			

Recommended dressing:
*Frothy Dressing
(see page 125)*

To serve:
Crisp wafer biscuits

Reserve 4 strawberries for decoration, hull and slice
the remainder. Mix with the liqueur and a little sugar,
if liked. Spoon into 4 large wine goblets. Make frothy
dressing. Flavour with a further 15 ml/1 tbsp of orange
liquer if liked and spoon over. Make a small slit from
the tip of each reserved strawberry and balance on the
rim of each glass for decoration. Chill, if time. Serve
with crisp wafers.

Surprise Caribbean Fruit Salad

Serves 4

	Metric	Imperial	American
Slices coconut or ginger cake	4	4	4
Bananas	4	4	4
Lemon juice			

Recommended dressing:
Pineapple and Orange
  dressing (see page 124)

To decorate:
Toasted coconut flakes, Orange slices

Put a slice of cake in the base of individual glass dishes. Slice the bananas, toss in the lemon juice and pile on top. Spoon the dressing over and chill. Decorate with coconut flakes and orange slices just before serving.

Forest Fruit Salad

Serves 4

	Metric	Imperial	American
Packet frozen forest fruits	500 g	1 lb 2 oz	1 lb 2 oz

Recommended dressing:
Red Wine Syrup dressing
  (see page 125)

To serve:
Custard sauce, Sponge finger biscuits

Place the fruits in a glass bowl and leave until thawed. Pour over the red wine syrup dressing, stir gently and leave to marinate for at least 2 hours for the flavours to develop. Serve with custard sauce and sponge finger biscuits.

SALAD DRESSINGS

Some of the salads in this book have their own dressings, others use a basic oil and vinegar, or French dressing. This section contains recipes for all the recommended dressings used in the book as well as some variations to give a choice of flavours to complement the different salad ingredients. There are some wonderful dressings for dessert fruit salads too.

SAVOURY SALAD DRESSINGS

Basic Oil and Vinegar Dressing

	Metric	Imperial	American
Olive oil	45 ml	3 tbsp	3 tbsp
Vinegar	15 ml	1 tbsp	1 tbsp
Salt and plenty of pepper			

The quantities will obviously depend on the quantity of salad, but the basic 3:1 ratio is constant. This is the case for all the oil-based dressings given here.

Note: For **Oil and Lemon** dressing, substitute lemon juice and 5 ml/1 tsp grated lemon rind instead of the vinegar.

Basic French Dressing

	Metric	Imperial	American
Olive oil	45 ml	3 tbsp	3 tbsp
Vinegar	15 ml	1 tbsp	1 tbsp
Mustard	2.5 ml	½ tsp	½ tsp
Sugar	1.5 ml	¼ tsp	¼ tsp
Salt and pepper			

Mix well together with a fork before pouring over the salad. Different flavours can be obtained by using English, French, Dijon, German or American mustard.

Basic Vinaigrette Dressing

	Metric	Imperial	American
Olive oil	45 ml	3 tbsp	3 tbsp
Vinegar	15 ml	1 tbsp	1 tbsp
Mustard	2.5 ml	½ tsp	½ tsp
Sugar	1.5 ml	¼ tsp	¼ tsp
Chopped onion	5 ml	1 tsp	1 tsp
Chopped fresh parsley	5 ml	1 tsp	1 tsp

Mix well together before pouring over the salad.

Sherry Dressing

Two-thirds sherry to one third vinegar in usual oil and vinegar combinations.

Variations on Basic Oil and Vinegar Dressing

Add one of the following:
- *10 ml/2 tsp mixed chopped parsley, marjoram and thyme*
- *10 ml/2 tsp mixed chopped parsley, gherkin and olives*
- *5 ml/1 tsp mixed chopped (snipped) chives and tarragon plus 2.5 ml/½ tsp mustard*
- *2.5 ml/½ tsp Worcestershire sauce and 5 ml/1 tsp chopped onion*
- *5 ml/1 tsp chopped mint*
- *5 ml/1 tsp chopped anchovies*
- *15 ml/1 tbsp crumbled blue vein cheese*
- *2.5 ml/½ tsp curry powder plus 1 sieved hard-boiled (hard-cooked) egg yolk*
- *Lemon juice instead of vinegar*

Basic Mayonnaise

	Metric	Imperial	American
Egg yolk	1	1	1
Olive oil	150 ml	¼ pt	⅔ cup
Wine vinegar	15 ml	1 tbsp	1 tbsp
Dry mustard	2.5 ml	½ tsp	½ tsp
Sugar	2.5 ml	½ tsp	½ tsp
Salt and pepper			

Whisk the yolk with all the other ingredients except the oil and vinegar. Add oil drop by drop, whisking all the time. Finally stir in the vinegar, drop by drop. Season if liked.

Note: You can substitute a good quality commercial mayonnaise if you prefer in any of the recipes.

Variations on Basic Mayonnaise
(These can also be added to bought mayonnaise.)

Add one of the following flavours:
- *10 ml/2 tsp chopped capers and chopped pimiento*
- *60 ml/4 tbsp whipped cream*
- *10 ml/2 tsp chopped (snipped) chives and parsley*
- *5 ml/1 tsp tomato ketchup (catsup) and paprika*
- *15 ml/1 tbsp crumbled blue cheese*
- *5 ml/1 tsp curry powder*

Cheese Mayonnaise

	Metric	Imperial	American
Cream cheese (or crumbled blue cheese)	100 g	4 oz	½ cup
Salt and pepper			
Prepared mustard	5 ml	1 tsp	1 tsp
Olive oil	30 ml	2 tbsp	2 tbsp
Milk	30 ml	2 tbsp	2 tbsp
Vinegar	30 ml	2 tbsp	2 tbsp

Beat the cheese until it is smooth. Work in a little salt and pepper and the mustard. Then gradually beat in the oil, milk and vinegar, one by one.

French Cream Dressing

	Metric	Imperial	American
English mustard	2.5 ml	½ tsp	½ tsp
Pinch of curry powder	1	1	1
Pinch of dried tarragon	1	1	1
Olive oil	30 ml	2 tbsp	2 tbsp
Single (light) cream	45 ml	3 tbsp	3 tbsp
Vinegar or sherry	30 ml	2 tbsp	2 tbsp

Mix the mustard, curry powder and tarragon with the oil. Gradually add the cream and beat. Then add the vinegar or sherry drop by drop, beating all the time.

Soured Cream Dressing

	Metric	Imperial	American
Hard-boiled (hard-cooked) eggs	2	2	2
Carton of soured (dairy sour) cream	150 ml	¼ pt	⅔ cup
Dash of tarragon vinegar			
Salt and pepper			

Sieve the egg yolks and mix to a smooth paste with the soured cream. Add a dash of vinegar and season to taste. For an interesting texture add the finely chopped egg whites at the end or use as a garnish with fresh chopped parsley over the finished salad.

Note: To make **Yoghurt Dressing**, substitute natural (plain) yoghurt for soured cream.

Garlic Dressing

	Metric	Imperial	American
Olive oil	30 ml	2 tbsp	2 tbsp
White wine vinegar	15 ml	1 tbsp	1 tbsp
Garlic clove, crushed	1	1	1
Salt and pepper			

Place all of the ingredients in a screw-top jar and shake well. Chill to blend flavours.

Honeyed Italian Dressing

	Metric	Imperial	American
Olive oil	60 ml	4 tbsp	4 tbsp
Lemon juice	30 ml	2 tbsp	2 tbsp
Parmesan cheese, grated	25 g	1 oz	¼ cup
Honey	15 ml	1 tbsp	1 tbsp
Dried oregano	2.5 ml	½ tsp	½ tsp
Salt and pepper			

Combine the ingredients in a screw-top jar and shake well. Chill to blend flavours.

Piquant Salad Dressing

	Metric	Imperial	American
Mayonnaise	45 ml	3 tbsp	3 tbsp
Lemon juice	30 ml	2 tbsp	2 tbsp
Honey	15 ml	1 tbsp	1 tbsp
Prepared mustard	1.5 ml	¼ tsp	¼ tsp
Pinch of paprika			

Combine all of the ingredients in a screw-top jar and shake well. Salt and pepper can be added if desired. This dressing is particularly good over tomatoes, cucumber and lettuce.

Oriental-style Dressing

	Metric	Imperial	American
Prepared mustard	2.5 ml	½ tsp	½ tsp
Sugar	2.5 ml	½ tsp	½ tsp
Sesame oil	30 ml	2 tbsp	2 tbsp
Soy sauce	15 ml	1 tbsp	1 tbsp
Black pepper			

Mix all of the ingredients together in a screw-top jar and chill before serving. A good pinch of ground ginger can also be used.

Green Onion Dressing

	Metric	Imperial	American
Mayonnaise	120 ml	4 fl oz	½ cup
Natural (plain) yoghurt	60 ml	4 tbsp	4 tbsp
Spring onion (scallion), cut into 3 cm/1 in lengths	1	1	1
White wine vinegar	10 ml	2 tsp	2 tsp
Chopped fresh parsley	5 ml	1 tsp	1 tsp
Pinch of sugar			
Pinch of salt			
Pinch of cayenne pepper			
Garlic clove	½	½	½

Place all of the ingredients except the garlic into a blender. Process until the onions and parsley are finely chopped. Squeeze the garlic over the mixture through a garlic press. Cover and chill for 1 hour before use.

DESSERT SALAD DRESSINGS

Pineapple and Orange Dressing

	Metric	Imperial	American
Sugar	1.5 ml	¼ tsp	¼ tsp
Grated orange rind	5 ml	1 tsp	1 tsp
Soured (dairy sour) cream	60 ml	4 tbsp	4 tbsp
Unsweetened pineapple juice	60 ml	4 tbsp	4 tbsp
Lemon juice	2.5 ml	½ tsp	½ tsp

Mix the sugar and orange rind and add to the soured cream. Mix in the pineapple and lemon juice.

Note: For more texture, add a can of crushed pineapple too.

Sugar-free Dressing

	Metric	Imperial	American
Small can apricots in natural juice	220 g	8 oz	8 oz
Apple juice	60 ml	4 tbsp	4 tbsp
Orange juice	30 ml	2 tbsp	2 tbsp

Purée the apricots in a blender or processor or by passing through a sieve (strainer). Stir in the apple juice and orange juice and chill until required.

Frothy Dressing

	Metric	Imperial	American
Can evaporated milk (chilled)	190 g	6½ oz	6½ oz
Lemon juice	30 ml	2 tbsp	2 tbsp
Caster (superfine) sugar	50 g	2 oz	¼ cup

Whip the evaporated milk until thick and frothy and almost doubled in bulk. Whisk in the lemon juice and sugar. Chill if liked before using.

Wine Syrup Dressing

	Metric	Imperial	American
Red or white wine (according to fruits used – red for red or purple fruits, white for other coloured fruits)	300 ml	½ pt	1¼ cups
Granulated sugar	75 g	3 oz	⅓ cup
Lemon juice	15 ml	1 tbsp	1 tbsp
Piece cinnamon stick	2.5 cm	1 in	1 in

Put the wine in a saucepan. Stir in the sugar until dissolved. Add the lemon juice and cinnamon stick. Bring to the boil, reduce heat and simmer gently for 10 minutes. Leave to cool then remove the cinnamon stick. Chill until ready to use.

INDEX